THE
Hidden Voice
OF
AFRICA

Sebastian Joseph

PARTRIDGE

To order additional copies of this book, contact
Partridge India
000 800 919 0634 (Call Free)
+91 000 80091 90634 (Outside India)
orders.india@partridgepublishing.com

www.partridgepublishing.com/india

I am also a human being. Let me live as a human being.

Open yourself to a glow of love for the whole world.
If you are unsure whether this book will harm you or help you, the
intent is to enrich your humanity and liberate you from
your fearful mind, to become a good leader of people.

LET YOUR HEART CATCH FIRE....

I dedicate this book to

All the African leaders and the people of Africa, including African diaspora around the world who are dreaming and working together to build a better African continent, to fulfill their forefathers' dream of a United States of Africa.
Let the Dark Continent blaze with light to be a colorful continent.

Love to you all
Sebastian Joseph
Author

- In the beginning, I was born on earth.
- All life on earth came from me.
- Among all I birthed, there was a very different kind of creature, called humans.
- I cared for them, granting wealth and abundance.
- Neither I as a continent nor my children have coveted or stolen from others. But many humans from other places came to my home and robbed me and my children.
- My powerful sons were slaughtered, taken captive, and exiled.
- My daughters were taken away from me to the auction market, where they were displayed topless, and all parts of their bodies were measured.
- They used my young daughters and mothers for sexual pleasure.
- They sold my children into slavery and exiled them to different continents.
- They used my children's backs as their seats.
- They spit into my children's mouths.
- My children were valued less than their dogs, for centuries.
- My educated children have become their toys.
- They used religion and religious leaders to make my children fight each other for the political benefit of the exploiters who wanted my wealth to steal and export.
- Now they decide whether my children should eat or not, and they decide what my children should eat and when.
- Yet the oil of the world is the oil of the lamp, the food for all my children, and the ornaments of their adornment.
- I am here to protect you. "I AM AFRICA."
- But my children don't understand—why?
- My children still live as their slaves—why?
- My children do not embrace their power for themselves and for future generations—why?

Contents

About This Book xiii

Chapter 1   This is Africa 1
Chapter 2   Human Rights 7
Chapter 3   Africa's Past 17
Chapter 4   Is Africa Rich? 21
Chapter 5   Assets in Africa 26
Chapter 6   From BPL to BPL 31
Chapter 7   The Religious Game in Politics 39
Chapter 8   Stop Begging and Fight for Your Rights 42
Chapter 9   Is Africa Poor? 49
Chapter 10 Child Military in Africa? 58
Chapter 11 Is The United Nations Supporting Justice? 63
Chapter 12 To My People in Africa 73
Chapter 13 How Do I Start a Business? I Don't Know How! 78
Chapter 14 Dream, Dream, Dream! 85
Chapter 15 How to Develop Africa 90
Chapter 16 The True Leaders on The African Continent 100
Chapter 17 Why Africa Got Freedom 111
Chapter 18 To The Young Generations in Africa 119
Chapter 19 The United States of Africa (African: USA) 127

About This Book

The world is now in the hands of mentally ill, warmongering fanatics. They have less conscience than cruel wild animals. They spend money to create powerful weapons that can destroy the earth in the blink of an eye. Because of their power, less than 10% of the world's population has a prosperous, comfortable life. The rest of the world is sacrificed for the convenience of these people, who make up 10% of the population.

Planet Earth is not the sole property of just a few people. We are all born into the world with equal rights as humans. The earth itself does not discriminate between white skin or black skin. The white man should not be considered superior, and the black man should not be considered inferior. White and black are products of geography, not of merit. When we came into this world, we brought nothing with us, and when we die, we will take nothing with us. During our lifetimes, peace is stolen from us in the world because of impatience, pride, and domination. If we fail to question these injustices, how can the next generation live here?

For more than 400 years, the African people have struggled with white colonialism, starting with the Portuguese. African communities lost not only their assets, but also generations of ancestors through slavery and oppression. Even today, the African community is spread across the world as diaspora, struggling for their rights without getting any respect, even though the vast resources of their continent have been looted by colonialists. Less than 5% of colonialists have spoiled the credibility of the rest of the good white people around the world, with the support of 2% of the Black colonialists. Their greed is a bottomless pit, and they never believe they have enough money.

Europeans who had nothing but ice to eat and only mountain caves to sleep in came to Africa and looted the continent. Colonialists, now you are eating 5-star meals which Africans are supposed to eat, and you are sleeping in the bungalows and mansions where Africans are sup posed to sleep, yet your hunger and greed still continue. The Congo River should be sufficient to supply drinking water to the whole African continent, but you will not allow that because of your political agenda to spoil the country's economy by continuing to loot minerals and met- als—gold, copper, cobalt, nickel, uranium, etc.—with the approval and support of a United Nations-controlled peacekeeping force. With those looted treasures, you have made your houses and streets colorful, leav- ing Africa a poor and dark continent.

I would like to point out that in the past, the world had cannibals because they had nothing else to eat. If you take everything away from Africans, you will make them cannibals again, and if that happens, the first thing they will eat will be white people—and you alone will be responsible for that. Africans have been forgiving for 400 years, but it is time to stop trying their patience. You distribute funds to divide and destroy Africa so that your own precious deadly weapons can be used in Africa and the Middle East. The time has come, and now the African people will unite, and you can no longer stop them. Now is the best time to stop Europeans' dirty games in Africa, which are modern colonialism.

In the news today, we see that people die of starvation during the race to become millionaires. Some people who have forgotten the truth of journalism celebrate births and deaths, their only goal being to make money. A man lives on this earth for a short time, and it is the good deeds he did while he was alive that will be remembered after his death.

Parasites will grow slowly on a large tree, but they will cover and kill the tree if we do not pay attention and eradicate the parasite early in its destruction.

I believe that this honest book will give essential knowledge back to each person, and that they can use this knowledge to create a better world, now and in the future.

May all human beings live happily on earth, die in peace, and pass on this legacy to the world through the next generation.

With lots of love,
Sebastian Joseph

CHAPTER 1

This is Africa

There are different kinds of animals in the African wilderness:

- Lions, tigers, leopards, etc.
- Hyenas, wolves, dogs, etc.
- Antelopes, deer, zebras, etc.
- Vultures, eagles, crows, etc.
- Rats, worms, bacteria, etc.

All of them want to hunt for food and enjoy the company of their own kind. The predator animals might pray, *O God, while I am running be- hind my food, please protect me from sharp branches and sudden deep valleys, and bring me success, for it will be very shameful if I fail and return to my home without making a kill.*

In the meantime, a deer or antelope might pray, *While I graze for my food, protect me from predators until I fill my stomach and return home.*

In the end, per the law of the wild, the predator hunts an antelope or deer and lick and each the hot blood food and as much of the flesh as they want. They leave the rest, and then the next category—the scavengers—come.

Wolves and hyenas fight each other for their part, and then when the odor of decay is prominent, then come the scavenger birds, the vultures and crows. Finally, rats, worms, and bacteria have their portion and contribute to the process of decay.

Whose prayer will God hear? These prayers may not be answered, because this is the law of the wild, and that law will continue forever. But one good thing is that when the predator's stomach is full, they will not hunt again until they are hungry, and they will not be worried about tomorrow's food.

Each category of creature makes an effort to find food—which category do you fall into?

There are a few people in the world who are not happy no matter how much they succeed or what happens to them, but overall, people correspond to the categories of animals I've discussed above.

Some are hunters: They create their own ideas and put in time and effort to achieve their dreams and goals. They care for others and protect their territory. Good leaders are born from this category.

Some are transgressive consumers: They steal other people's savings and have no ideas of their own but want to enjoy success with no effort. They have no aspiration beyond their own benefit, and their hearts are hard.

Then there are those who hide and attack like with fox intelligence and python belly. These people are the real thieves, and we can see many of this type in politics—I don't mean the good politicians. These are the people who are cancerous parasites in every country.

And there are people with no desires of their own—this category is like lazy animals who have no dreams or goals, always waiting for someone else to feed them.

Which category do you fall into?

As the old saying goes, "There is only one difference between humans and animals: the ability to laugh. Some people laugh, like humans . . . and some people do not laugh, like animals."

He who has ears, let him hear. He who has a mind, let him use it to win back his kingdom.

I'd like to tell you a story to illustrate my point. Once upon a time, a team of thieves planned to hunt in the African jungle, using hidden weapons. For a few days, they didn't find anything other than small animals, and then they found a group of wild animals and their families. In the same area, they discovered precious metals, but they could not enter those areas to take what they wanted, because of the danger from the wild animals.

They started to attack the animals and killed as many as they could. Among that group, one man decided to catch a pair of tigers, which he gave to a zoo. Then he and the other men started mining, and they looted the assets from Africa and took those treasures to their homeland.

At the zoo, for a few days the male tiger would not eat anything, and he tried his best to escape from his cage. Each time he tried, he was struck a blow by the guards. The female tiger simply watched as her mate kept trying to escape, but failed. Months passed, and along with the other animals, they learned to be obedient and to eat what they were fed. A few months later, they had a baby tiger. For him, this zoo was like a pal- ace, and he began to enjoy himself with the other animals—he'd never learned about hunting, for he had never been taught to hunt in the wild. Again, the male tiger tried to escape, but again he failed and was punished in front of his wife and son.

One day the baby tiger asked, "Mama, why is my father trying to escape from us? We have food to eat and a place to sleep. Why is Papa like this?"

The mother tiger explained about the jungle, their freedom, and how much they enjoyed hunting when they were in the jungle. Just from listening to this, the male tiger's eyes were full of tears. At last, the tiger family decided to live peacefully, and together, they would play and do tricks for visitors.

A few years later, the zoo decided to sell the father tiger to a circus, because he was so obedient. He had forgotten life in the jungle and what it was like to be free. The thieves were still hunting in the jungle . . . **and the young tiger has never taken any action to escape with his mother from captivity in the zoo.**

This is the real story of Africa now. The present generation has never known what is Africa and forgotten to resist—their teeth are no longer sharp, and they have forgotten how to hunt.

Abraham Lincoln said if slavery was not wrong, then nothing was wrong—for nothing was more inherently monstrous than slavery.

Africans, it's time for you to rise up, to free yourself and liberate yourself from the leeches bleeding you dry. It is your turn to claim your assets and your own country. East Africa was controlled by the British and Germans, and then by the Portuguese and the Sultanate of Oman. East Africa was divided into two parts—German East Africa and British East Africa.

Each African must feel proud that you are still feeding Europe and America. Using your precious raw materials and resources, they become rich. In return, Africans get weapons to kill your own people, but they don't accept that. Yet still, they say that you are poor.

The port of Zanzibar was a primary destination for business tycoons, with the main export being spices—another name for Zanzibar was "spice land." The port also exported elephant tusks, with thousands of elephants killed during those days to take their tusks—the size of the tusks could be six feet or more, and they were exported to China, India, Iran, etc. for ivory manufacturing. Indians, Arabs, and local Zanzibaries participated in the biggest business of all: human slavery. Slaves were brought from Somalia, Sudan, Kenya, Uganda, Republic of Congo, Zambia, Malawi, etc. The main human slave market was called "Stone Town."

https://www.google.com/search?q=stone+town+old+pictures+wikipedia&rlz
https://anyexcusetotravel.com/travel/zanzibar-slave-market/

It was the old palace of the sultan, and if you want to visit the location, it is near the British-built Christ Church. From 1800 or before, until 1909, the slave trade was legal for rich people in East Africa and most of the world. **We must remember that the British Empire supported the abolition of slavery and paid compensation to slaveholders to free their slaves.** Stone Town is now a cultural museum in Zanzibar, where you can see the heart-wrenching statue of five slaves locked together with a chain, like dogs.

During British colonial rule, in 1906 Barghash bin Said was forced by the British to abolish the slave trade in the Zanzibar Archipelago. The end of the 18th century and the beginning of the 19th century saw the dawning of a golden age for slaves—more than ten thousand slaves were freed from their chains. However, human slavery continued illegally until the 1930s, with Indians, Arabs, and Zanzibaries participated.

On 9 December 1961, Tanganyika became an independent republic and in 1962 it became known as Tanzania.

Once, whites enslaved Africans. They still rule Black people today, but the difference is that they do so with the support of a Black colonialized mentality. Still, the assets and wealth are enjoyed by the white colonials only, and to this day, the slaves' loyalty to the whites remains.

In the 21st century, slavery continues in Asia, the Middle East and in some Arab countries, Africa, North America etc.

The following activities in any form qualify as slavery:

- Compulsory overtime work, exceeding national guidelines
- Denying rights to ordinary men and women
- Child labor by force
- Binding/shackling of limbs
- Denial of food/water
- Humiliation
- Sexual assaults
- Threats (especially of sexual abuse)
- Solitary confinement
- Beatings or any form of corporal punishment
- Exposure to excessive heat and cold
- Burning And much more…

When slavery was present, African slaves suffered even more than the outrages listed above. Those who purchased female slaves examined the women to make sure that they did not have sharpened teeth and that they were sexually pleasing. The buyer was allowed to touch any part of the slave's body.

If you visit Zanzibar, there is a presentation at the Stone Town museum that will bring tears to the eyes of any person with a heart. A six-year-old boy named Cypriani Asmani tried to escape from slavery and received a cruel punishment. A wooden piece weighing twenty kg was placed on his head and tied there with chains. He lived with that punishment for over a year.

In 1895, a missionary came to rescue him and freed him from this punishment. If a six-year-old boy was the victim of such heartless cruelty, you can imagine how much worse the punishments were for adult men and women.

Punishments are still given even before children are born, in parts of Africa, but they are now in a different form. However, the government leaders and the younger generations don't realize what is happening.

"The Truth About Slavery": White people were the first slaves. In 1659, the English shipped many Irish and Scots to Barbados as slaves. More British exiles were shipped after 1685 following the crushing of the Protestant-led Monmouth Rebellion in England. The link below explores and exposes the truth about the rhetoric that white people were slaves too, primarily Irish white slaves, referred to as "white cargo," and the white Barbary slave trade. It also addresses the assertion that because the Jews endured the Holocaust, Black people should "get over" the in- justices of slavery.

https://www.google.com/search?q=The+Truth+About+Slavery+-+White+ People+Were+The+FIRST+Slaves+-+LIES+Exposed...+ Exploring+and+ex posing

Human Rights

What you have today was in someone else's hands yesterday. What you have today will go to someone else tomorrow. You can make use only of what you have, today. Then why are you taking from others what they deserve? Do not forget that we are just of piece of "life" in this earth, it can sustain only for few years and no matter how much we have all must leave it here other than sole.

Everyone on this planet has an equal right to live. The earth has no inherent caste or religion—the planet doesn't care whether people are Black or white, rich or poor. Black and white people have the same blood and bodily functions. Then why are Black people enslaved simply because of the color of their skin? Is it because of their humility?

From Alexander the Great to Steve Jobs: The Same Message

After conquering many kingdoms, Alexander the Great was returning home. On the way, he fell gravely ill. On his deathbed, he called his generals and said, "I would like the world to know of the three lessons I have just learned." He took a deep breath, and said, "I will depart from this world soon, and I have three wishes. Please carry them out, without fail."

Alexander continued, "My first desire is that my physicians alone must carry my coffin. I want my physicians to carry my coffin because people should realize that no doctor on this earth can really cure anybody. They are powerless to save anyone from the clutches of death. So, let people not take life for granted.

"Second, I desire that when my coffin is being carried to the grave, the path to the graveyard shall be strewn with the gold, silver, and precious stones I have collected in my treasury. I spent all my life pursuing greed and power, earning riches, but I cannot take anything with me. Let people realize that chasing wealth is a sheer waste of time.

"My third and last wish is that both of my hands be kept dangling out of my coffin. I wish people to know that I came empty-handed into this world, and empty-handed I go out of this world."

With these words, the king closed his eyes. Soon, he let death conquer him and breathed his last.

When billionaire Steve Jobs passed away at the age of fifty-six from pancreatic cancer, he had a similar message. In September 2011, his net worth was $7 billion US.

His last words were: "I reached the pinnacle of success in the business world. In others' eyes, my life is the epitome of success. However, aside from work, I have little joy. In the end, wealth is only a part of life that I am accustomed to. At this moment, lying on my sickbed and recalling my whole life, I realize that all the recognition and wealth that I took so much pride in have paled and become meaningless in the face of impending death. You can employ someone to drive a car for you and to make money for you, but you cannot hire someone to endure sickness for you. In time, we must face the day when the curtain comes down."

Let us wait and see what the following richest people in the world choose to say before they die: Now they are in the competition of being the number one in the Millionaires/Billionaires list. I pray that you do not forget to eat and spend time with your wife and children during this first race.

2020: The Richest People in the World.
Forbes counted 2,095 billionaires for 2020, collectively worth $8 trillion.

#1 Jeff Bezos
#2 Bill Gates
#3 Bernard Arnault

#4 Warren Buffett
#5 Larry Ellison
#6 Amancio Ortega

2020: The Richest People in India

#1 Mukesh Ambani
#2 SP Hinduja & Family
#3 Gautam Adani
#4 Shiv Nadar & Family

2020: The Richest People in Africa

#1 Aliko Dangote (Nigeria)
#2 Nicky Oppenheimer & family (South Africa)
#3 Mike Adenuga (Nigeria)
#4 Nassef Sawiris (Egypt)

What change can these few rich people make in their lives with the money they own? Instead, the lives of many families would have been better off if these rich people had given up their comforts and savings for the next ten generations and given the rest to the employees of their establishments.

No one will take anything with them when they die, other than their soul.

Your soul came from somewhere when you were born, innocent and blank as white paper. As your life goes on, your deeds and character write on that paper, and your soul will walk away with this paper when you die. Remember, when your soul passes away from you, that paper, the record of your life, will be submitted for final judgment—it is you, and you are the only one to decide what will be written on it, and whether it will be pure or unclean. Your body is just a temporary place for your soul to stay for a while.

Each person is born only once and dies only once during their life-time—and the longest lives are between eighty and a hundred years, with many being shorter than that. This equals around 30,000 days or less, no matter how poor or wealthy you are. Each day has its own purpose. How you use it makes a difference. Everyone ends life in a wooden box or a white shroud, or they are cremated, or their bodies are left for few birds or scavengers . . . and that is all we take to the end.

William Shakespeare said, "All the world's a stage, and all the men and women merely players." No matter whether you are rich or poor, you will have happiness, disappointment, triumph, and sadness—everyone will have experiences and emotions. Everyone gets a role to perform, and you will be rewarded based on your performance. After the last show, the curtain comes down—that is our ending. Some people who do not understand this truth and try to pacify their own minds by holding everything in their hands without even giving others what they deserve. History does not seem to have given them peace of mind.

You are loved when you are born.
You will be loved when you die.
In between, you have to figure out how to manage.

Did you enjoy eating, sleeping, and spending time with your family today, no matter what you had to eat, or where you live? If so, rejoice, because you are rich today. Some of the wealthy people out there have billions in the bank and they have the most expensive mattresses and silk sheets, but they can't sleep. They have five-star meals, but they can't eat. A husband and wife can't sleep together; there are children and privileges, but there is no peace. So what is the point of accumulating excess wealth?

Some rich people want to be the wealthiest so they can say to the world, "I am the richest person in the world." It has been shown officially that the assets of the top twenty wealthiest people in the world could lift the world's population out of poverty and hunger. God has not offered the wealthy more than the normal human lifespan.

Is it possible to change an hour or a day in the book of your lifetime, with your money?

Some countries in Africa are rising up now, with the support of a few visionary leaders. Those who are the real leaders are determined to create change, even at the risk of their own lives or their families' lives. These are called revolutionary leaders. Also, the COVID-19 pandemic is an eye- opener for African people and African diaspora around the world. They have now realized that their true homeland is Africa, and that Mother Africa will accept her children anytime, without hesitation. The African diaspora have started supporting their true country with their hearts, now, because they have realized what a major role racism and White Supremacy have played in their lives, over years and years. Always remember that when you are diaspora, you are like a bird in a cage—you may have every comfort, but you lack freedom. Any diaspora in any country are treated like second- class citizens. You will have the privilege of being a first-class citizen only in your own country. So, if you have any chance to go back to your country of origin, you must go back and build your life there, so that the next generation will not kneel down in front of others.

Africa has been nominally free of colonial rule for more than forty years, yet most African countries are controlled by the same colonialists who used to openly rule. When they left, they put their own people in the top positions, to fulfill their goals, and this still continues. Those who could not do anything on their own like a parasite clung to other trees absorbed all the vitamins available to the tree and remained there until the tree was destroyed. The tree will not survive without cutting down some of these branches. This is the current situation in Africa therefore, Africa is still poor, because its resources and assets are still going to other countries, with the support of the present corrupt leaders.

A few good leaders are coming up in Ethiopia, Rwanda, Zimbabwe, Ghana, Sudan, Botswana, Namibia, etc.; which is the good sign for Africa's development.

The colonialists started developing rebel groups and depriving people of human rights, to spoil the country again. They are like a dog with a bone, in their determination to take what Africa has to offer. This is the truth about colonial rule in Africa:

- During the centuries of colonial rule, if human rights had been implemented and enforced, Africa would never be poor.
- What have colonialists done for Africa, other than killing people and making an entire generation hungry by depriving them of human rights?
- Who gave colonialists the authority to deprive Africans of human rights?

- Have they shown any compassion or humanity during centuries of colonial rule?
- How many millions of people were killed in the Democratic Republic of Congo and the Central African Republic by Belgium and France together? These are the richest countries in the world, yet their people are the poorest. The United Nations has had a presence for many years, but what humanitarian work are they doing, other than supplying a few food items? At the same time, thousands of tons of gold, copper, cobalt, and diamonds have been looted from those countries.
- Technology has been developed to take detailed pictures of outer space, and yet somehow, the United Nations still cannot identify the thieves who are looting Africa's assets.
- Is the presence of the United Nations really meant to protect the African people? Or does it protect the thieves?
- If colonialists believe in human rights, why are they looting Africa's assets? Why are they supplying weapons to Africa and training children to fight against their own country and people?
- African leaders know their people, and they know how to control the people who are perpetrating illegal activities. These issues are internal to Africa. No one has the right to deprive a country of human rights, especially in the developing countries of Africa.
- When colonialists show concern for human rights in undeveloped countries, and countries at civil war, then the African people will trust that you care about human rights and justice.
- Africa's intelligence and integrity are far greater than those of colonialists.
- When colonialist rule fails, that is when they say there are human rights violations.

Leave Africa to be ruled by its own leaders—let those leaders lead their own countries. They don't need your support. Because of centuries of colonial rule, and colonialists' lack of respect for human rights, Africa never reached its potential. Let's consider the example of the "mercy"

Belgians showed to the Congolese. When the Congolese did not meet the Belgians' standards by bringing enough resources to them from the jungle, the punishment was to cut and bind their children's hands and feet. But now the Belgians think they have the authority to talk to Africans about human rights?

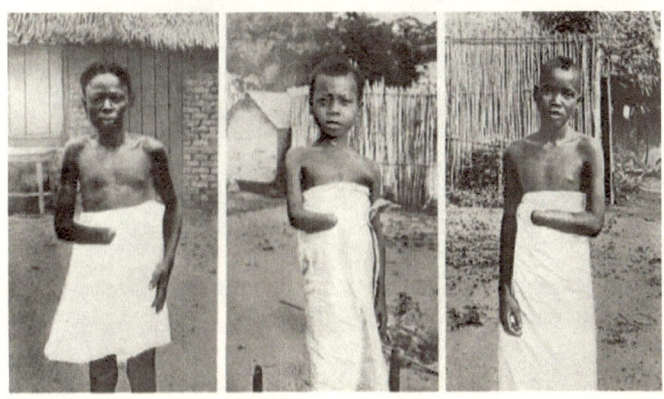

A father stares at the hand and foot of his five-year-old daughter, severed as a punishment for having harvested too little rubber.

https://www.google.com/search?q=belgium+congo+punishment&rlz=1C 1NHXL

Humanitarian legacy of white colonialism still continuing in Congo.

Belgium begins to face the brutal colonial legacy of Leopold II

President Paul Kagame of Rwanda was interviewed several times by European journalists. Their questions focused on human rights, but it seemed that each journalist would ask questions and then answer without giving President Kagame a chance to answer. The president silently listened for a while, and then pointed out that the journalist was ask- ing the question and then answering it to prove that the president was wrong—and that it was wrong to interview him and ask questions with- out even allowing him to answer. Yes, Africa needs powerful leaders like Paul Kagame. Africa has a lack of strong leaders. President Kagame recently deported eighteen Chinese citizens from Rwanda for human rights violations, a decision that clearly said, "Enough is enough—we don't want any other country to colonize Rwanda." This is an additional jewel to add to his presidential crown.

Nelson Chamisa, the Zimbabwean politician and the current President of the Movement for Democratic Change, made the same point during his presidential election campaign interview at Oxford University in London. He has said that our country and its people have suffered under the oppression of white colonialists—enough is enough, and we do not want any more colonial activity in Africa. The people of Zimbabwe are now well educated and know how to handle our country and its people.

Now the competition in Africa is between the Chinese and the Europeans. For centuries, these countries have squeezed the juice out of Africa, and Africa realizes that. Now, Africa will not interact with Europe or China except in partnership—not at the mercy of so-called "philanthropy." Africans need their rights and protections. They want to improve their lives; they are the heirs of Africa, and they want a better life, just like any other people on any other continent. This is what the African people deserve.

Remember: People throw stones to dislodge fruit only from abundantly bearing trees.

<u>**Below is a sample summary of Africans killed or lost to colonialism.**</u>

Congo: Since 1580, under the regime of Belgium and France, millions of Congolese people have died. Modern estimates range from one million to fifteen million, with a current consensus of around ten million.

Central African Republic: Since 1870, under the oppression of Belgium, France, Great Britain, and Germany, more than 581,362 people have been internally displaced.

Namibia: There is no agreed-upon figure regarding how many people have died since 1884 at the hands of German colonialists, but some estimates have put it as high as 100,000. It is thought that three-quarters of the Herero population and half of the Nama population have died.

Somalian Republic: The British and internal civil wars have taken tens of thousands of lives since 1920. Various sources estimate the deaths to be between 50,000-100,000 while local reports estimate total civilian deaths to be upwards of 200,000 Isaaq.

Throughout the African continent, millions have been murdered or lost—some estimate that as many as 10 million people have died.

CHAPTER 3

Africa's Past

"God bestowed all the nations of the world with many blessings. But in Africa alone, the blessings still have not come. Africa asks: Let us live as human beings. Please"

Africa is the birthplace of humankind, and knowing its history is essential to understanding the global society that has grown around it. In the past, there were no distinctions of race or color in Africa. Instead, it was a tribal culture. Each tribe identified with its own members and had its own boundaries. The tribes clashed with each other and banded together; they lived happily like a mother and children.

The eldest family member ruled as the leader. He was respected by all members of the tribe, and his word was law. Tribal culture had no concept of cheating or stealing. Every mother was a mother to all; each child belonged to all mothers, and the children lived together. When a mother made a meal, all the children went home to eat—each child was valued equally, and that is essential to African culture.

Africa is very good at being hospitable to guests. Africans are humble and generous, and they assumed that other people were the same. This is what allowed others to take advantage. Portuguese, Europeans, American and Arabs took advantage of this humility and began to invade Africa and confiscate property and resources.

(It continues to this day that Africans are gifted with white and black Gods that they do not know about, and that humans are pitted against each other in the name of Gods and religion, and that their assets and humans are plundered. Do the Gods hate Africans so much? Which has plagued them for more than five hundred years. Are Africans destined to beg only from the rich who plunder so much wealth in Africa?)

For centuries, these tyrants enslaved and ruled Africa. Those who opposed the colonialists were brutally executed, and healthy young men and women were enslaved and sold to other lands. The women fell victim to colonialists' lust, and then the oppressors took their children from them. The colonialists are like a fox between two rams, which beat their heads together to crush the fox and drink its blood. Those who were taken as slaves sailed away in ships and were forced into labor that even animals could not do. The kings and queens of Africa became slaves in many countries.

British colonialism ruled over Africa for centuries. They captured the strongest men in the world as their slaves and shipped them to territorial colonies to do agricultural work in America, Europe, and parts of Asia. Some of the young African women and mothers were sold to Arab countries.

WHO MADE AFRICA POOR?

Slave Trade in Africa

A lithograph, circa 1880, of a group of men, women, and children being taken to a slave market

The transatlantic slave trade began during the 15th century when Portugal, and subsequently other European kingdoms, were finally able to expand overseas and reach Africa. The Portuguese first began to kidnap people from the west coast of Africa and take those they enslaved back to Europe and America. The slave trade became a business for colonialists in Africa, including Europeans, Asians, and Arabs, and it continued until the end of the 19th century. A few African countries, such as Liberia, Ethiopia, were not targeted for the slave trade. This is one reason why Ethiopia has an advantage over other African countries regarding politics and education.

Those exiled into slavery never saw their family or home country again. The tortured cries of these men still echo around the world. This anguish continues today in many parts of Africa. Until the 19th century, only the enslaved suffered brutality because of human slavery. But when the whites learned that Africa is rich in natural wealth, slavery started again in the form of exploitation, all over Africa.

The Slave Trade

Enslaved Family

Children being taken to a slave market.

Now, White colonialism and Black colonialism work together to export Africa's wealth to different parts of the world. As a result, Africa is still enslaved.

Is Africa Rich?

Yes indeed—fifty or sixty years ago, most of the African continent was richer (collectively, of course—exact conditions varied among countries) than India, China, and the Middle East. They built six-lane high- ways, the world's longest bridges, and schools, colleges, factories, etc. In those days, some African countries exported food products, cotton, sugar, livestock, oil, minerals, precious stones, etc. to Asia, the Middle East, Europe, and America. Sudanese and Nigerian currency value was almost equal to the British pound sterling. Even today, this wealth is still abundant in Africa, but the current generation does not see it, and the forces behind it are not giving Africans the opportunity to benefit from it.

During those days, many professional people—teachers, professors, engineers, tech workers, etc.—came to Africa for jobs and business opportunities. During the time of British colonialism in India, the brutality of the British became unbearable. From 1900 to 1930, many people from the southern part of India escaped with their lives to African countries such as Ethiopia, Sudan, Tanzania, Kenya, and Uganda, and from there, some of them escaped to different parts of other African countries.

More than 70,000 Indian families live all over Sudan, but the majority live in a state called Kassaala. They have become Sudanese nationals and married one another, living peacefully with their own businesses and jobs.

Recently, the United States and Russia have been conducting operations, which I would call catastrophic oppression, in Syria. Many families have lost their relatives, and those who were able fled as refugees to Africa. The Sudanese welcomed them and supported them like family. Some of these families are also in the faming business.

No matter how wrong the children are, the mother forgives—and following that example, Mother Africa waits patiently.

The richest man in the world in the 14th century was an African, Mansa Musa, who was richer in his time than Jeff Bezos is in the present day. Mansa Musa was an emperor in Mali from 1312 to 1337. His net worth in today's terms would be 400 billion dollars. The present-day richest man in the world, Amazon founder and CEO Jeff Bezos, is worth 149.3 billion as of 2020.

Mansa Musa's vision was not to enlarge the size of his country, but rather, his focus was on improving his people. He founded schools, universities, and libraries. He had a collection of more than a million books, in the 14th century. He welcomed guests from many other countries.

As an example of his luxurious life, Mansa Musa made a pilgrimage from Mali to Mecca, a distance of around 6500 kilometers. He was accompanied by over 1000 camels, who wore flattened carpets. There were two soldiers on each camel, their equipage made of gold. Musa completed his pilgrimage journey in two years, accompanied by countless people. To travel from one end of his retinue to the other took about three days. He threw gold on his way to Mecca, to help the poor people. On his journey, he gave an order to build a mosque each Friday.

This was a bad time in Mali, because thanks to this trip made by Mansa Musa, the French realized that Africa had vast wealth in gold. During this time, Mali and its territorial African countries were rich, but most of the European countries were living in caves due to the cold weather and struggling for their daily bread. When they found out about the gold mines in Africa, the French colonialists conquered Mali, and within a few years, Mali became the poorest country in Africa. The

French conquerors looted the country and sent all the wealth to France. All of Mali's territories became French colonies.

During the war between Germany and France, Germany took over those assets and brought them to Germany. Later, during World War II, the Americans and Russians were victorious over Germany and then the Americans and Russians shared that wealth.

Yes, Africa was rich, and will be rich again if Europeans do not interfere with them anymore, and Black colonialism ends.

In those days, European colonialists were roaming the world like a hungry fox. We can't blame them for this, because they were trying to survive, just like wild animals do. They took their ships and went to Asia and Africa, the lands of greatest promise. The countries hunting for wealth included Great Britain, France, Germany, Portugal, Italy, Spain, Belgium, China etc. Most of the colonies were established by the British, including the North American continent. In a way, we can say that colonization was not a crime—in those days, people's mindsets were different. Even some of the Arab countries did the same to survive, and their main income source was robbery. This is mentioned in both the Holy Bible and the Quran.

Those days are gone, but the colonialist behavior continues, and it is no longer understandable or excusable. You may be wondering how this is possible—but believe it or not, the Western world still controls most countries in Africa. That is the power of Black colonialism all over

Africa. Have you noticed that political leaders are quickly getting richer and richer, having big investments in Europe and America?

Remember, the tree that grows too fast can quickly crack down the middle—all it needs is a windstorm. The windstorm that breaks the bad tree must be the common people of the land. They must destroy the tree whose roots sap their land; the longer it stays, the stronger it grows, and it will be very difficult to uproot later.

Alhaji Aliko Dangote

"Africa is full of opportunities." This is a valuable observation from the remarkable Aliko Dangote.

The richest man in Nigeria and 23rd richest man in the world in the 21st century, Alhaji Aliko Dangote GCON is a Nigerian businessman and philanthropist who is the founder and chairman of Dangote Group, an industrial conglomerate in Africa. Unlike other Africans, he did not re- locate his money and assets to another country. He proudly invested his money in business in his own land. More than 25,000 job opportunities have been created because of his kind generosity, and he has promised to expand job opportunities to around 180,000 in five years. Every African who is participating in Black colonialism, making money off the backs of their own people, should look at this example of how to think and live like a lion, not like a fox. If all Africans acted as Dangote has done, then with the support of its own government Africa would rise like a phoenix from the ashes to create a strong economy, and no one would be hungry again.

Aliko Dangote was born on April 10, 1957 in Kano State, Nigeria. He was born into a wealthy family. At the age of eight he lost his father. Humility and simplicity are Dangote's trademarks. He borrowed money from his uncle to start a business after he finished school. From there, he continued his business journey into trade, agriculture, refineries, and manufacturing of cement, sugar, food products, and more.

Nigeria is one of the biggest oil exporters in the world, but unfortunately, there is no refinery to feed domestic consumption of oil products. Soon his vision will come true. One of Dangote's visions is that Nigeria must be self-supporting to produce all the petroleum products that the country needs. Dangote spread his wings and expanded his businesses into more than sixteen African countries, buying mining licenses. He invested all his money into African businesses—yes, his money is not hiding somewhere in a bank; it is being used to benefit his people.

Of 180 countries, Nigeria is the 146th least corrupt, according to the 2019 Corruption Perceptions Index reported by Transparency International. A corrupt leader must realize that when you contribute to corruption, you are spoiling your own and your family's name; you are also corrupting your country and your homeland. You must realize that stolen money will not give you any kind of comfort, because you will know that you are guilty. The game you are playing is only hide and seek; if you steal money through corruption in Nigeria and hide it in a European or an American bank without doing anything with it to benefit your African brothers and sisters, at the end, your soul will still take nothing with it when you say goodbye to this world.

Below is a list of African countries and their most prominent natural resources. If these resources were pooled for just five years, Africa would be the richest continent in the world. All African countries must put an end to or severely limit foreign companies' oil and mineral extraction, and over a period of fifteen years, those countries must pay 50% of their profit share to each government. Africa is the continent from which the most minerals and resources are extracted, yet the trillions of dollars of profit do not benefit her own children.

Tanzania: Diamonds, gold, iron, nickel, uranium, tanzanite, oil, gas
Guinea: Diamonds, gold, bauxite, aluminum, iron

Mozambique: Gold, precious stones, aluminum, tantalum, coal, iron, oil, gas

South Africa: Diamonds, gold, platinum, copper, uranium, iron, vanadium, nickel, oil, gas

Ghana: Diamonds, gold, bauxite, silver, manganese, oil, coca Zambia: Gold, copper, lead, zinc, uranium, cobalt

Namibia: Diamonds, uranium, zinc, lead, Sulphur, copper, tantalite
Niger: Gold, uranium, coal, phosphate, iron, oil

Nigeria: Gold, diamonds, iron, coal, lead, zinc, oil, gas

Democratic Republic of Congo: Diamonds, gold, copper, cobalt, iron, lithium, lead

This list could go on and on . . . .

CHAPTER 5

Assets in Africa

Until the 19th century, Europeans had little firsthand knowledge of Africa. Many African countries are rich with natural resources.

Hydrocarbon: Oil and Gas

Some of the African countries found and explored oil (the years cited are approximate)

- Somalia, 1948
- Angola, 1953-1975
- Nigeria, 1956-1967
- Sudan, 1959-1983
- Democratic Republic of Congo 1970-1997
- Tanzania, 1973-1978 (and recently it discovered natural gas)
- Kenya, 2012

There are many more examples.

Africans could not enjoy long years of oil production, even though the quality of their oil supply is far better than that of other countries. Within a few years of the discovery of oil, civil wars and political crises started in most African countries. Thousands of people were killed or injured/handicapped, and a majority of them became homeless. The richest African countries are now poor, with most people struggling for their daily bread. That was the condition of Europe until the 14th and 15th centuries, when they started looking past their own resources and began to colonize African, Asian, and Middle Eastern countries. Young African men and women have now gone to other countries to make a living and take care of their loved ones.

The saddest part is that some African countries are still discovering oil, gold, diamonds, and other minerals, but either they don't have proper refineries or the government will not maintain them. They export crude oil and then import petrol, diesel, etc. from other countries for domestic use, at a higher cost than if they were operating in-country re- fineries. **There may be some hidden reason for this, which benefits political leaders—and recently you might have heard that millions in foreign currencies were discovered in the house of a certain president in Africa.** If refineries were fully functional in these countries, the cost of electricity would be drastically reduced; if electricity were available, the manufacturing companies would also see improved function. When manufacturing is doing well, imports will decrease, and the GDP (Gross Domestic Product) will increase. **The political leaders of these countries are conspiring together to share the benefits, and not supporting the development of their countries. There are countries in Africa that pay more for finished petroleum products than they make from exporting crude oil.**

Below is a list of minerals, precious stones, etc. to be found in Africa.

The African continent is rich with minerals. These are some of the countries where these resources can be found:

- Botswana: Diamonds/kimberlite, gold, silver, copper, precious stones
- South Africa: Diamonds/kimberlite, gold
- Somalia: Gold, copper, iron
- Nigeria: Gold, copper, iron
- Sudan: Gold, precious stones
- Egypt: Gold, copper, precious stones
- Tanzania: Gold, copper, precious stones

- Burundi: Gold, copper
- Mali: Gold, copper, precious stones
- Central African Republic: Gold
- There are many more examples.

Until now, camels and donkeys were walking on top of these assets in many countries.

Each year, thousands of tons of these resources are produced from African countries and are taken by European or other foreign manufacturers. Most of the time, these assets never reach the government; instead, they are illegally exported to other countries. None of the local African people get any benefit. Just imagine, if one year's worth of stolen precious metals or gemstones was accounted for to the government, African countries would be rich in their per capita income (the average income earned by a person in a given area—city, region, country, etc.— in a given year, calculated by dividing the area's total income by its total population). But unfortunately, you can see the majority of these countries' people living in small huts, or homeless in the streets.

It's time to wake up and smell the coffee—it is your turn now. Stop colonialists from looting your assets from your own land!

AGRICULTURE

Africa is blessed with the two longest rivers in the world—the Blue Nile and the White Nile and their branches, which cover almost all the countries in Africa, supplying water to its wilderness and its people. The fertile land does not require any fertilizers to produce the maximum yield of crops. Wherever you throw seeds and water, they will grow. Africa is the only continent which is still largely free of pollution.

The majority of the agricultural cultivation areas are empty due to poverty or lack of governmental support. Conditions would be much improved if governments would plan ahead and invest a bit— for example, an area may not be close enough to the river, and the government could provide solar-powered water pumps to support agriculture. Most countries get seasonal rain and need only initial support to cultivate the land and buy seed to support the farmers. This would be a good opportunity for the people as well as the government to create exports to boost the economy.

Some countries produce animal feed and export it to different countries, but the governments and people who do so are not thinking clearly—rather than exporting animal feed, that same feed could be used to farm more animals in their own country. They could then export meat to other countries at a far greater profit.

European countries prefer African fruits and vegetables due to the much lower levels of pollution/contamination. Africa's food products are not poisoned, and the Europeans know the value of unpolluted food; they know how pollution and radiation are absorbed into trees and plants where there are factories.

Unfortunately, some African countries import even such staples as potatoes and onions from other continents.

Yes, this is true. Africa does not produce what it consumes—it exports what it produces. Botswana and Namibia export over 20,000 tons of meat, but its neighboring countries are struggling for meat. In Kenya, tea is planted in an area of over 157,720 hectares, with production of about 345,817 metric tons of tea, of which over 325,533 metric tons will be exported. Then it is processed in European countries, labeled by the processors, and returned to Africa. Tanzania, Kenya, Senegal, and Zambia produce millions of tons of cashew nuts, but the lion's share is exported to India and Europe for processing and labeling by the processors, who then claim country of origin. These are only a few examples.

There are many other products exported from Africa for processing. It would not require much investment to create processing capacity in Africa, but it requires governmental leadership that can think ahead and organize, so that job opportunities will increase for African children, and the country will earn more by exporting finished products rather than outsourcing the processing. Nigeria, the biggest exporter of oil in eighty-four countries, doesn't have enough refineries to process the oil. They export crude oil and bring back petrol, diesel, kerosene, etc. for domestic usage. This is the only country where you can buy petrol much more cheaply than kerosene.

Don't underestimate African leaders—they know what can be done in their own country, but if they do, they cannot support the colonial- ist agenda and make themselves rich. Remember, only ten producing farmers are required to feed a thousand families.

Eliminate poverty by putting your hands to your own land to produce food for your own people to eat—not only is it good economic policy, it is a moral responsibility. Some people do farm, but they don't care about their neighbors or poor people. Let me illustrate my point with a small story.

The fertile land of a certain wealthy man produced crops, and he said, "This is what I will do. I will tear down my barns and build larger ones. And into these, I will gather all the things that have been grown for me, as well as my goods. And I will say to my soul: Soul, you have many goods, stored up for many years. Relax, eat, drink, and be cheerful."

But God said to him, "Foolish one, this very night your soul is re- quired of you. To whom, then, will these things belong which you have prepared?"

Thus it is with him who saves worldly goods for himself and is not wealthy with God or with the poor. This story comes from the Holy Bible, Luke 12:15-20.

If God gives me more than I ever dreamed of, I must never think that it is only for me and my family. I must always share with those who are really needy, because no matter how strong and intelligent people are, we are incapable of extending life for even a day. We are more than just a tool in God's hand. When our earthly comforts increase, we forget our souls.

Even the cruelest animals in the forest fill their bellies and leave the rest for other creatures, but some human beings do not show their fellow humans the mercy shown by these wild animals. If you are reading this, I am sure you are not in this category.

Every day, humans become more and more selfish. Genuine love is confined to only a few people.

If you would like to start a small business with an affordable initial in vestment, look into a joint venture with farmers. This area of business has little interference from bad political leaders, because they do not like to visit places where there is hard work, dust, and dirt.

## CHAPTER 6

From BPL to BPL

From Bad Political Leaders to Below Poverty Level

WARNING!!!

Dear reader, if you are a Bad Political Leader (BPL, or A-Team), either stop reading, or hand over this book to someone who hates you. By learning about yourself and who you are, there is an increased chance that you may lose control, lose your sanity, or become suicidal. The writer of this book is not responsible for any of your actions.

If you are in the category of Below Poverty Level (BPL, or B-Team), you had better open your mind and soul, to have a chance of getting to the next level of Above Poverty Level (APL), or you should stop reading and hand over this book to someone who loves you, because opportunity will not keep knocking indefinitely. Being an African man or woman, you have a sleeping lion within you to resist and protect yourself, or the A-Team will continue to oppress you and use you as their slaves.

If you want to climb a mountain, you will have to climb at least one hill.

No one brings anything with them when they are born from their mother's womb, whether rich or poor, and no one will take anything with them from this earth, to heaven or to hell.

You remain poor because you don't want to change yourself. You don't find anything because you are not looking for it. You do not get your rights because you do not ask for them. You are not achieving because you are not dreaming.

Your dreams do not come true because you are not working on them. You remain slaves because you continue to bend your backs to the A-Team.

Without doing things correctly, you can continue to pray to God, but He will never answer you, because God has given you a brain to think, and a body with which to take action, and God may have priorities other than what you might prefer. So do your duty perfectly, and pray to God for blessings.

If God created you in His image, why are you still a slave?

Humans are the only creatures that are ruining the earth today. Each country has more than a hundred times the food the country itself needs, but 10% of the population owns all that wealth. The major role played by the A-Team is to pop up during the election and come out of their cages to mingle with the B-Team by promising many things and spouting slogans. Once the election is over, most of the leaders will not be seen again until the next election.

This drama is common not only in Africa, but also in most of the continents in the world. In this context, the main actors are the A-Team, who joint venture (JV) with big business. These are the people controlling the other 90% of the population. I don't want to describe politics in further detail, because these are common factors in every country, and you are already experiencing them. Most of the time, the BPL-JV uses religion as their weapon, all over the world. India's BPL-JV is the number one predator among all the countries. In some Indian states, the religious game plays the role very well, mostly where people are uneducated and there is little development. In those areas, they treat some groups of people as if they are worth less than a cow. They are even ready to kill people in order to protect the cow. Does the cow know anything about this? I don't think so.

On the other hand, India is one of the biggest exporters of beef all over the world, especially to the Middle East, China, Europe, and America. It is a real joke, because India has a lot of religions, as well as castes, tribes, and different ethnicities. The most prominent racial apartheid in the world happens within India's religions, even today.

The caste system divides Hindus into four main categories: Brahmins, Kshatriyas, Vaishyas, and Shudras. Many believe that the groups originated from Brahma, the Hindu god of creation. The members of different castes must keep their distance from each other, based on hierarchy.

Making up roughly three percent of the population, they are the third- largest religious group in India, after Hindus and Muslims. The Indian Christian community includes about 17 million Catholics and 11 mil- lion Protestants. Many Christians are tribal, or members of lower castes such as the Dalits (the Untouchables).

When we consider population, there are around 182 million Sunni, Shia, and Ahmadiyya (Ahmadiyya Muslim Community or the Ahmadiyya Muslim Jama'at is an Islamic revival or messianic movement founded in Punjab, British India, in the late 19th century). By a 2017 estimate, India's Muslim population is about the world's third-largest and the world's largest Muslim-minority population. India is home to 10.3% of the world's Muslim population.

Therefore, in India, there is no difficulty in picking a religious bullet during elections.

Recently, you may have noticed that over sixty Indian millionaires/ billionaires have escaped from India to Europe, the UK, and America by cheating the Indian banks, with the support of BPL-JV. The Indian government had mercy on them and wrote off all those debts, but the loans taken out by poor farmers to buy seed and prepare the land for farming are still due, resulting in the suicides of more than 6000 farmers, due to foreclosures and destruction of farmland by natural disasters. The BPL-JV devils laugh.

Did God ask you to fight each other, in any holy book?

All other countries may have one or two religions, such as Islam and Christianity, but here again, the BPL-JV can play their game more easily. They make the two religions fight each other. This dirty game happens more in the African continent, and Team B will be defeated here.

Again I ask: *Did God ask you to fight each other, in any holy book?*

Where there are only Muslims, here is another joke—they make Sunni and Shia Muslims fight with each other. This dirty game is happening in the Middle East and on some parts of the African continent.

Did Allah, or any messenger of Allah, ask you to fight each other, in any holy book?

Where there are only Christians, there is still a hidden killer—the role of White Supremacy in the BPL-JV game. White Supremacy plays a major role in conflict among Christians on almost all continents, but especially Europe, North America, and Africa.

Jesus Christ or any of His disciples ask you to fight one another in the name of God?

If you don't know about White Supremacy, I recommend the book *Me and White Supremacy* by Layla F. Saad—author, speaker, and podcast host on topics of race, identity, leadership, personal transformation, and social change. Her book has been on the *New York Times* bestseller list twice. You can buy it online in either a UK or a USA edition. It is also being translated into many other languages.

This is not a fictional book—it is the true story of the bitter experiences she has undergone as a Black Muslim woman, daughter of East African immigrant parents to the United Kingdom, from Kenya and Tanzania. Even as a British citizen, she has suffered from racism.

When Saad started an Instagram challenge called #Me and White Supremacy, she never imagined it would spread so quickly. Using a step-by-step reflection process, she encouraged people with white privilege to examine their racist thoughts and behaviors. Tens of thousands participated in the challenge, and more than ninety thousand people downloaded the *Me and White Supremacy* workbook. Since then, the work has spread to families, educational settings, nonprofits, corporations, and more.

Based on the original workbook, *Me and White Supremacy* teaches readers to understand their perceptions through the lens of White Supremacy so they can stop inflicting (often unconscious) damage on people of color, and in turn, help other white people to do better, too.

At this time in history, more than ever before, people are asking what they can do to help dismantle White Supremacy and where to begin. Layla F. Saad answers: "Begin within, begin with you and White Supremacy."

No matter who you are—African, European, American, or Asian— it is a must-read. Now Saad's blog has over a million followers, whom she is enlightening about White Supremacy. The majority of them are white people from Europe and America. The reason for this is that current generations are more educated, mature, and kind—they don't want to be like their forefathers, who created the most inhuman system imaginable, to protect themselves from Black slave uprisings.

Why does BPL-JV use religion as a weapon?

This strategy imitates British white colonialism, because Europeans, especially the British, controlled countries on nearly every continent for many centuries, especially in Asia, the Middle East, and Africa. Their policy is "divide and conquer"—religion is still the most powerful weapon to divide people, though none of the holy books call for people to hate other religions or kill each other. All holy books focus on a message of love, peace, sharing, caring, mercy, and more—the message is to read your holy book every day, to become a better person, not to fight for God. When you are a better person, you will never consider harming people, regardless of religion, caste, or color, and you will also never question or criticize other religious beliefs.

The main agenda of the religious fight is to divide and spoil the economy or the country itself, through the support of the A-Team and JV. When there are religious wars, there will be a demand for weapons, which are mostly manufactured by the colonialists, Russia, America, and Europe, who are also the managers of the United Nations, although that organization has 193 member countries. The majority of the African countries' wealth will be used to procure the weapons. The same support will provide for both countries without their knowing it. The weapons manufacturers are selling the weapons deals—also another joke. One group will sell missiles, and another group will sell a weapon to block the missiles. By that time, the country's valuable wealth, such as precious metals and stones, or oil and gas, will be looted with the support of the A-Team. When there are wars between countries, that is when the greatest profit accrues to those who make weapons. They produce and export to those who are fighting for them, pretending to help that country. These extremely destructive weapons will land on that country's factories, residences, hospitals, roads, etc. and will kill the people or make them into refugees.

This game is most prevalent in the Middle East and Africa. The current examples right in front of us include Iraq, Iran, Libya, Syria, Yemen, Somalia, Sudan, Republic of Congo, and more. **Note: these are all re- source-rich countries.**

There are other poor countries with civil wars and political problems— why aren't the weapons manufacturers helping them? It's because the countries don't have the money to procure weapons, so please make note of the fact that the motivation here is not to help the country—all these people want to do is sell their weapons and make a profit.

If you are an African, do you really want your country's valuable assets—gold, diamonds, oil, and much more—to be looted from your country every year with the help of BPL-JV? Do your due diligence to research the following countries: South Africa, Sudan, Nigeria, Mali, Burundi. They produce tons of gold every year. Botswana, Mali, and Burundi mine countless diamonds every year, and yet the local people are paid only in pollution and disease. The news quote below is only one example of the value of diamonds:

"TORONTO – Lucara Diamond Corp. has unearthed the largest uncut diamond in recent history in its Karowe mine in Botswana, the Canadian company said, beating its own record discovery from November 2015 that it struggled to sell for nearly two years. The 1,758-carat diamond, larger than a tennis ball, weighs close to 352 grams (12.42 ounces), Lucara said in a statement. The stone is second in size only to the 3,106-carat Cullinan Diamond, recovered in South Africa in 1905.

"The stone is the latest in a series of high-value recoveries for the com- pany at Karowe. Since introducing its XRT diamond recovery technology, Lucara has recovered 12 diamonds over 300 carats, including a 472-carat and a 327-carat diamond in April 2018.

"The 1,109-carat Lesedi La Rona, which Lucara recovered in November 2015, failed to meet its undisclosed reserve price at a June 2016 auction, putting pressure on the company's shares. British diamond dealer Graff Diamonds finally bought it for $53 million in September 2017."

If the good leaders of African countries would plan wisely and retain just one year's worth of these assets, their country's GDP would sky-rocket and they could get a loan from the World Bank against these accumulated assets to obtain equipment and build facilities to mine their own resources.

A country's development starts with a good leader. This can be an everyday citizen, or a professional politician. But that person must have standards.

If a mother is not capable of feeding her child, she knows that she is not a good mother.

If a husband is not capable for taking care of his wife and children, he knows that he is not a good husband or a father.

If a political leader of the country is not cable of feeding his people, he must say that he is not a good leader and leave that position. If he does not, he is part of the A-Team, and the country will never prosper.

Sometimes, good leaders will be trapped by the A-Team/JV, which may offer two options to control that leader:

Option One: Do what we say, and your family will be happy and pro- tected forever.

Option Two: If you rebel against us, your family will be killed, which is already happening in many countries—in India, for example, the good police officers and judges are frequent victims.

The majority of leaders will choose the first option. They can't help being afraid for their own safety and that of their family. But there have been leaders who have risked it all to do the right thing: Fidel Castro, Mahatma Gandhi, Martin Luther King Jr., Nelson Mandela, Abraham Lincoln, and more. They were willing to risk their lives; they know that each man is born only once and dies only once. Even though they died, they died as kings, and the world still respects them. Their names are written in gold. How many of the rich people's or bad political leaders' names will be remembered? They died in love with their money, with corrupt reputations, and they died like wild animals. Even a dog will not remember them a few years after their death, and their children do not love them.

"What good is it if you gain the whole world and lose your soul?" If you are a Bad Political Leader (BPL/A-Team), this is for you:

➢ You are a traitor, like Judas. Because of you, your family and country were spied on.

➢ Your kingdom has perished because of you.

➢ Your people are starving because of you.

➢ Because of you, your people are disgraced and have no clothing.

➢ Because of you, your people are homeless, sleeping on the street like animals.

➢ You destroyed your rich country through collusion with colonialists.

➢ You have opened the door for other thieves to ruin your country.

➢ Along with others, you have called your land a poor country.

One day you, like Judas, will commit suicide without peace.

If you think your children will enjoy the wealth you have stolen, you are mistaken....

That money is a tomb for your children.

Remember, if your looted earnings are just a few millions, that is equivalent to a cyanide capsule in your neck. If you have more than that, then your entire body is covered with a suicide bomb that may explode at any time. That is your lack of peace.

What do you do with your money? You send it to European or American banks to hold it, but after a few years, you will die, and then your children will not be able to bring this money back to your country.

The financial crisis of 2007-2008 led to many bank failures in the United States. The Federal Deposit Insurance Corporation (FDIC) closed 465 failed banks between 2008 and 2012.

Those bank failures represented several years of African, Middle Eastern, and Asian looted funds. The closure of those banks served a purpose: you cannot claim that money.

CHAPTER 7

The Religious Game in Politics

Most new political leaders use religion as a weapon all over the world during elections, especially in less-educated rural areas, where the most votes can be gained. When the politicians fail to deliver on their promises and cannot hide their incompetence, they take out their religious weapons so that the people will fight each other, focus on religion, and forget their leaders' mistakes. Subsequently, these political devils smile and enjoy their comfort zone.

Do you ever see political leaders or their children on the front lines of religious conflict?

Because they don't want to die, they will send you to the religious battlefield to die for them. Regardless of your religion, you have to wonder why you are willing to die for them. When you die, you and your family are the losers. If their belief is stronger than yours, then they must be on the front lines of the religious battlefield. If the political leaders had even 10% belief in God, they would never mix religion and politics, because regardless of which religion it is, our forefathers did not create it for material benefit—religion is intended to unite people. God sent His word through proverbs and prophets to make our minds and souls better. If your mind and soul become good, you will get along with others. Remember, when you die, you will take nothing with you from this earth—not even your body. Religion is your faith and belief; your mind is controlled by your soul, and your soul should be controlled by God. If it's not, you must be prepared to meet the devil when you die.

If faith could bring wealth through prayer, there would be no poverty. You can see that the majority of poor people in Africa and India pray more than the rich people do, but they stay poor. You may notice that most of the churches in Europe and America have been converted to performance spaces, bars, etc. In Christian churches, even on Sundays, you can count on both hands the number of people attending to worship. The real believers will never flaunt their belief in front of anyone, because they know that belief is for the soul—no matter how rich or poor you are, in front of God, your soul will be measured, not your wealth or your physical body.

If we believe that all humans were created by God, that means the per- son in front of you was also created by God—so how can you hate the people in front of you? If you want to do something for God, do some- thing for the person in front of you, and give thanks to God. Don't fight in the name of religion.

Why are you using religion as a reason to fight for God? Who are you to protect and fight for God? Are you the savior of God?

The most prominent religious leaders live in five-star facilities and command poor people to pray to God. This is particularly prevalent in extremely religious countries such as Somalia, Sudan, South Sudan, Nigeria, Central African Republic, Republic of Congo, Ethiopia, Syria, Libya, Egypt, Iran, Iraq, Yemen, etc.

- Why does religion seem to support certain political leaders, so that they fight one another for their seats?
- Why does religion support some pastoral ministries in the practice of becoming celebrities, to whom the poor give away their money, leading these people to take money as donations and live in luxury?
- Why does religion cause poor people to remain poor?

If you do not agree that religion is doing these things, then answer these questions:

- Why are these countries still struggling with war and poverty after many years?
- If God and religion are protecting them, then why are these countries still so poor?
- You may note that these countries are rich in natural resources—but why are the people not enjoying their wealth?
- There are many churches, mosques, and home retreat centers being established every day. Why are those religious leaders not taking any action to stop colonialists from looting assets from African countries and pumping all the assets into Europe, China, and America, if they really believe in God?
- These people have been praying for more than five hundred years. Why is God ignoring their prayers and supporting the thieves?
- When people are about to die of hunger, they may lose their patience and start an uprising. That is when religious leaders tell them that God will protect them and punish the thieves—but why is it not happening?
- Without the support of religious and political leaders, nothing will change in these countries.
- It's inarguable that other countries are taking advantage of this situation by weaponizing religion, regardless of what religion it is.

Always remember that God's priority is not to give you material wealth. God is concerned only with your soul, no matter whether you are rich or poor, and God has given each person a brain to think with and a body with which to take action. God will not hear your prayers unless you do your duty. God's priorities may be different from yours.

Stop Begging and Fight for Your Rights

When you work for an employer or a company, you get paid—that is your right, and you are not at the mercy of your employer's whims regarding whether you should be paid. But when you work for the government, that is referred to as "service," because you are a servant of the people and the government. You are paid from taxes, which is money paid to the government from people's income or consumption of goods. Taxation is supposed to be equitable for all citizens.

Likewise...

If another country enters your country and takes action to remove an asset, you must be aware of what is going on and insist on your rights, even if you don't have the resources to develop those assets yourself. You are eligible to receive a higher percentage of profits than the investor will receive. They should not be paying you because they are sorry for you—you must be aware of the fact that you are doing them a favor by letting them into your country and working with them. Your forefathers, who were so kind and opened the door for them without knowing what they were doing, gave them power to rule over you for centuries. You are well educated now, so you must use your ability to think before allowing anyone to enter your country to take your wealth.

Do you worry that you don't have enough capital to mine and refine your resources? You don't necessarily need your own funds. There are many investment and exploration companies that can help you to extract and refine your own resources. But to do that, you must present a plan that is well thought out and credible to others. You should check with one of the larges exploration companies in the world, which will help you to find your assets and bring investors to develop your country, with minimal investment:

GeoResonance Pte Ltd. www.georesonance.com
Middle East and Africa:
Contact: sebastian@georesonance.co
Sebastian Joseph

GeoResonance Technology performs unique geophysical surveys to search for hydrocarbons, minerals, ground water, and artifacts. With over twenty years of experience in geophysical surveys, the company offers a unique and proven methodology of subsurface exploration.

GeorResonance Technology unmistakably identifies subsurface sub- stances and their characteristics using spectral signatures. The surveys are unambiguous, fast, and cost effective. Since 1997, the company has successfully completed more than 100 survey projects over 156,000 square kilometers on five continents, including Africa and the Antarctic Peninsula. GeoResonance Technology has been used to find hydrocarbons, ground water, and deposits of gold, copper, uranium, nickel, and platinum—as well as other precious and base metals.

The effectiveness of the technology has been proven by drilling and trials. The following is a small selection of projects for various commodities around the world:

Canada—gold; Somalia—iron ore; Mongolia—oil and gas; Mexico—gold; USA—oil and gas, shale gas; Australia—oil and gas; Indonesia—oil and gas; Iran—ground water; Nigeria—oil; Turkey—geothermal and offshore gas; Vietnam—titanium; Russia—coal; Republic of Congo—diamonds.

You can see many more references at www.georesonance.com

GeoResonance remote sensing surveys are based on proprietary processing of multispectral satellite images of the survey area. Vast areas can be comprehensively surveyed within weeks. The remote sensing survey reliably identifies hydrocarbons, minerals, and ground water to 5000-meter depth.

You just need to spend a little money to buy a hook to catch the big fish. That is what white colonialism is doing, to locate and loot the assets from your homeland.

You may ask—"How can I do that?"

If a king is good, then the people will be better off. This is the basis of change needed in Africa.

You have to attract investors and seek advice from countries with natural resources similar to yours. However, nearly any other country's re- sources are minimal compared to Africa—for example, a country may have only oil and gas, but Africa has oil, gas, diamonds, gold, copper, silver, nickel, platinum, iron, agriculture, wilderness, etc. Forty years ago, some Middle Eastern countries were untapped, like Africa, but now they are among the richest countries in the Middle East—especially Qatar.

By 1971, the termination date of the British treaty relationship was approaching, and accordingly, Qatar declared its independence on September 3, 1971. Qatar is a small, credible, non-corrupted country. The citizens never think about corruption, because they are well taken care of by the government. They are paid well and have a quality of liv- ing far above only basic needs. They have free education, free medical care, free land and homes. Regardless of whether a citizen is educated or not, they will get a job from the government according to their capability. However, Qatar promotes education and sports, and the government supports students to obtain the highest degree of education they want, at government expense.

There are more Qatar expatriates than there are citizens. The expatriates are also well taken care of by the government, with pensions, free medical care, etc.

Qatar is a country of 11,571 square kilometers, with a population close to three million. The GDP of Qatar is expected to reach USD 201 billion by the end of 2020, according to global macro models and analysts' expectations. In the long term, the Qatar GDP is projected to trend around USD 207 billion in 2021 and USD 212 billion in 2022, according to econometric models. Qatar's most significant natural resources are petroleum and natural gas. The revenues from oil and natural gas in 2007 helped it to achieve the world's highest per capita income.

Shell started seismic surveys (by the way, GeoResonance's precise, unique exploration technology is far better than seismic exploration technology) in the Qatar waters in the spring of 1953. They drilled two exploratory wells in 1955 and 1956, but both wells were dry. It was only in May 1960 that Shell discovered the Idd al-Sharqi oil and gas field, some 85 km east of Doha.

In 1997, Khalid Gazal began exporting LNG when it sent 5.7 billion cubic feet (160 million cubic meters of LNG to Spain. Qatar has become the world's leading LNG exporter, next to Australia. In 2009, Qatar exported nearly 1.8 trillion cubic feet (51 billion cubic meters) of LNG, with Japan, South Korea, and India as the primary destinations.

Qatar has become one of the premier tourist destinations in the Middle East. In 2018, the total number of hotels in Qatar was 110, including hotels in all categories, from five-star luxury hotels to one-star hotels. If you are a tourist, you must come to Qatar to see how they have changed the desert into a paradise. There are wonderful tourist destinations, including Qatara, Pearl Qatar, Souq Waqif, and the Qatar Museum.

The Museum of Islamic Art is at one end of the seven-kilometer-long Corniche in Doha, Qatar. Per the specifications of the architect, I.M. Pei, the museum is built on an island of an artificial peninsula projecting from the traditional dhow harbor.

Banana Island is a small island in Qatar. Its territory is crescent-shaped, and it is located off the coast of the capital city of Doha. It is an artificial island in the Persian Gulf. Anantara's Banana Island Resort Doha was built there. The island covers 13 hectares and has its own marina and reefs.

The Qatar government encourages all types of sporting events, especially football. This is a link to football stadiums for the FIFA World Cup 2022.

https://www.stadiumguide.com/tournaments/fifa-world-cup-2022-stadi- ums-qatar/.

All five stadium projects have been designed by German architect Albert Speer & Partners. The air conditioning in the stadiums, for both players and spectators, will be solar powered, carbon neutral, and provided by Arup of England. Qatar will be the first West Asian nation and also the smallest country ever to host a FIFA World Cup, with unique attractions, and spectacular state-of-the-art venues. Under its proposal to FIFA, Qatar will build nine new stadiums and renovate three, with the twelve venues divided among seven host cities: Al-Daayen, Al-Khor, Al-Rayyan, Al-Shamal, Al-Wakrah, Doha, and Umm Salal.

To promote sports and education, Qatar started a sports school, Aspire Academy (www.aspire.qa). The Aspire Dome is the largest indoor multi-purpose dome in Qatar. It is located at Aspire Academy in Doha and has the capacity to host thirteen different sporting events simultaneously, in a climate-controlled arena, in addition to having a full-sized indoor football pitch. Qatar is also a leader in education, with the Qatar Foundation for Education, Science, and Community Development, a semi-private chartered non-profit organization founded in 1995 by then-emir Sheikh Hamad bin Khalifa al Thani and his wife, Moza Bint Nasser.

The Supreme Committee for Delivery and Legacy (SC), which over- sees the organization of the upcoming FIFA World Cup 2022, is aiming to sell three million tickets to achieve its target of having full stadiums for every match during the world's biggest sporting event, which expects to receive more than 1.5 million football fans from around the world.

This development and growth happened in less than twenty years, be- cause the government of Qatar, and their advisory board, were good managers of the income from their natural resources. They managed these assets without corruption, and with honesty, integrity, and loyalty to the people of Qatar. In effect, Qatar is one of the richest countries in the world.

The 2006 Asian Games, officially known as the XV Asiad, was an Asian multi-sport event held in Doha, Qatar from December 1st to 15th 2006, featuring 424 events in 39 sports. Doha was the first city in its region and only the second in West Asia to host the games.

Charity begins at home. Yes, Qatar believes that all people have an equal right to live in the world, so they take care of their citizens first, and then move into the wider world to help the neediest. Qatar is number one in the field of charity, with Qatar Charity, an international charity organization. It was established in 1992 for the development and sustainability of needy communities across the globe. Qatar Charity has helped many African countries. A few years before, Qatar built many homes for poor people, especially widows in Sudan Bahari. They also built hospitals and schools as part of their charitable work in Sudan, as well as in other African and Arab countries.

There is an old Chinese saying: "One good turn deserves another." Africa is missing this.

Africa had and still has more natural resources than Qatar—so why is Africa struggling? Even before Qatar, they found oil and minerals. The reason is corruption—and corruption is the motto of the leaders guiding Africa's future. This corruption is in support of the same colonialists who ruled over them for centuries. **"Once a dog sees a bone, the dog will stay until he gets it."** The corrupt leaders think only of themselves and their families. Only a few African countries are exploring and mining oil and minerals, even though almost all African countries have one or more reserves of natural resources. Every year, how much oil, gold, and other resources are taken from Africa? And yet, Africa is still poor and begging for help from other countries—because begging is easy. The bad leaders in those countries make their people beg. Those leaders don't want to use their brains to figure out how they can develop their country. Their main agenda is looting of assets, with the support of the Western world, and establishing a life of luxury for their families. They don't care what happens to anyone else. Africa is poor, and yet each of the fifty-five African countries is rich in highly valuable natural resources.

We need a new generation of revolutionary leaders. Maybe you will be among them? Yes, the young, educated generation can restore wealth to Africa, taking to the next level the work of the old leaders who worked against colonialism: **Nelson Mandela, Jomo Kenyatta, Julius Kambarage Nyerere, Robert Mugabe, Thomas Sankara,**

Kwame Nkrumah, Patrice Lumumba, and others who fought for freedom from white colonialism to get Africa back.

In the 21ˢᵗ century, Africa lacks leaders of this caliber, and therefore the majority of African countries are forced to beg for support from the United Nations and other countries. To change this, the African leaders must emulate the example of the government and rulers of Qatar regarding management of assets. Africa must seek advice from countries like Qatar to learn how best to support development. It's certain that Qatar will never reject a request for advice, because Qatar's vision is to improve the world without jealousy, and they are already supporting African countries.

No matter how much the white colonialists have already looted from Africa, the natural resources are still sufficient to make Africa flourish within just a few years.

With the natural resources from your country and good leadership, none of your citizens will ever have to beg for help from other countries.

Is Africa Poor?

The white colonial system labeled Africa as "poor," to discourage the rest of the world from discovering Africa's riches. White colonialists and the United Nations have spent millions of dollars on disinformation campaigns to highlight Africa's supposed poverty. If they had spent 10 percent of that advertising money on Africa itself, that would be enough to feed poor families not only in Africa but around the world.

White colonialists come with "aid packages," supplies by organizations such as UNICEF, the Red Cross, Red Crescent, etc.—almost all of which are European creations. They may show you pictures of poor, unhealthy children close to death, with their mothers—these pictures are designed to get donations from countries and individuals for these charitable organizations. The link below will show you a typical example.

https://www.google.com/search?q=Africa+the+poor+with+their+mother%2C&tbm

ARE THEY NOT GOD'S CHILDREN? WHAT SINS HAVE THEY COMMITTED IN THEIR LIVES? WHY DOES GOD NOT TAKE CARE OF THEM? WHY DOES GOD NOT LISTEN TO THEIR PRAYERS?

This dynamic has been in place for more than a hundred years. You may also see aid in the form of food supplies thrown from airplanes into the jungles and related areas of the Central African Republic, Congo, South Sudan, Nigeria, and more.

https://www.pinterest.com/formaner/ how-poverty-affects-children-in-africa/

WHO IS RESPONSIBLE?

THE REAL OWNERS OF THE GOLD AND MINERALS ARE THE AFRICAN CHILDREN WHO ARE STARVING TO DEATH.

https://www.google.com/search?q=Africa%20the%20poor%20un- healthy%20children%E2%80%99s%20near

Behind this dirty game, millions of dollars are taken from Africa. In these same regions, you will note a high incidence of civil war, child abuse, and human trafficking. These are the same areas where mining and exploitation of natural reserves occurs; the aid packages benefit not the poor people, but the colonialists who are robbing them.

Africa does not require any of your free food or aid—Africa needs you to stop colonialism. After seeing the human cost of stealing Africa's wealth, how can you keep doing it? How hard is your heart? When are you going to stop this brutality? You say that Africa is poor—but you are looting their assets and making them poor.

It is a simple fact that no European countries, except for Russia, have gold. So why is the gold reserve in Europe higher than it is in Africa?

More than $500 billion derived from African gold and other minerals is deposited to the French Central Bank and other European banks every year. And yet still the United Nations and colonialist countries say that Africa is poor?

This gold is from Congo—is this country poor?

https://africanminingmarket.com/uganda-risks-becoming-hub-for-gold- smugglers/3367/

This gold is from Uganda—is this country poor?

https://africanminingmarket.com/congos-gold-being-smuggled-out-by-the- tonne-un-report-finds/7143/

These are only two examples—there are many more.

These resources are all stolen from Africa. If colonialists purchased these resources officially or gave Africa their fair share, then Africa would be the richest economy in the world, with a GDP higher than that of any other country. But the criminal organizations that steal from Africa will never allow these poor people to live peacefully.

If the United Nations, or UNICEF, or related organizations really want to help these areas where thousands of families suffer, how much mon- ey would be required, and how long would it last, to provide good food and shelter?

The same drama was seen during British colonialism in India. They came with their excess food products to give the impression that they were helping the poor, and then their ships returned to Britain filled with iron, coral, spices, and other raw materials for which they had not paid a single dollar. They told the people that they needed these items as ballast weight to balance the ship for safe passage.

These so-called charitable acts are packaged in flashy photographs and film—but they are criminal acts nevertheless. One ton of donated food is purchased by looting one ton of gold from Africa.

You can see gold being looted if you follow this link:

https://www.google.com/search?q=gold+smuggling+in+africa&tbm =isch&ved=2ahUKEwjHufi-

This is the ultimate result of these charitable organizations. You should just spit on them when they offer aid—someday, all the assets of your country will be yours, and then you will never beg again.

Africa was not poor in the distant past. Due to a long history of colonial- ism, Africans have forgotten what their lives were like before colonial- ism and slavery. When Europeans were caged by cold weather and lack of opportunity, Africa was the richest continent, controlled by its own emperors. Look up the history of Egypt, Ethiopia, Ghana, Zimbabwe, etc.—these countries were rich in the days before Christianity. Europe has made Africa poor by controlling its wealth from behind the scenes. They claim that Africa is poor because they have a political agenda to loot Africa's wealth.

The current generation of Africans still has not identified the potential reserves of Africa. Africa is not poor, but the mentality of the people is that of poverty. If Africa were poor, why would the Arabs, Portuguese, Germans, British, French, Italians, and Asians flock to colonize it? Why have they been in Africa for 600 years like bees to honey? The legacy of 600 years of exploitation has led to the United Nations and others coming to Africa with food and aid packages because Africa is "poor."

The fruit-laden tree will bend to the ground, and it is easy for anyone to jump into that tree—that is what happened to Africa!

Because your African ancestors were kind, and their hearts were pure, they did not realize that these thieves had come to conquer Africa and her children. Yes, Africa is poor now because of colonialists, so please stop bothering them—get out of Africa with your aid kits and your exploitation, and then Africa will rise and fly on her own.

Sudan: To the Greeks, from Homer onward, all people living south of Egypt have been called Ethiopians, inhabiting the areas now known as Sudan and Ethiopia. Later, Sudan as far south as Khartoum became widely known by the Latin name of Nubia. Northern Sudan's earliest historical records come from ancient Egyptian sources, which described the land upriver as Kush, or "wretched." For more than two thousand years, this was the Old Kingdom of Egypt. From 2010 on- ward, the Sudanese government gave permission to private citizens to find gold, at their own expense.

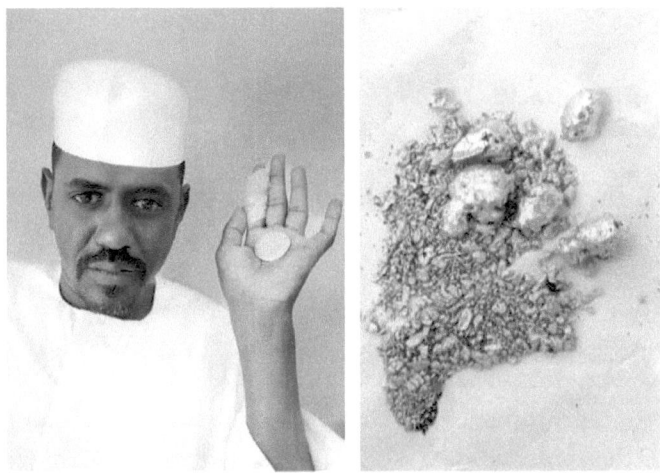

Suliman Al Mehady, the Sudanese gold farming
investor for poor gold farmers.

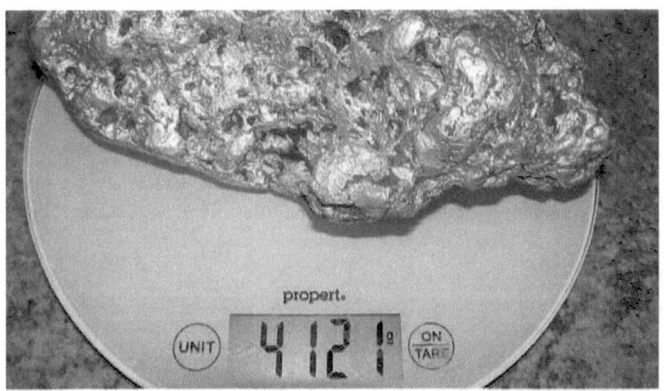

This gold nugget, 4121gm, was found as one piece in Sudan.

These gold farmers who have found gold through their own efforts
are given permission to sell that gold to the government at the current
international standard price.

Gold stone-crushing area in Sudan (witnessed by Sebastian Joseph together with El Hadi Abdurahman Mohammad Ahmed).

Some of the luckiest gold farmers become millionaires because of this permission from the government.

This gold nugget, weighing 17 kilograms, was found as one piece in Sudan.

Sudan is the only African country from which the colonialists have not taken much gold, so the gold reserves in Sudan are still tremendous. In other African countries, colonialists have mined tons of gold, copper, cobalt, uranium, tin, nickel, diamonds, aluminum, manganese—every mineral and gem you can think of, looting billions of dollars every year. In those areas, the colonialists protect their territories with soldiers—if you attempt to cross those lines, you will be killed. The world does not know this hidden secret, that colonialists identify mineral assets and loot billions of dollars every year, while they show photos of poor people, to give the impression that Africa is poverty-stricken. Yes, there are many poor people in Africa . . . but they are poor because of colonialists.

In Sudan, the government officials stationed at the mining areas purchase gold from the gold farmers and give a payment voucher which can be used immediately to collect cash from the bank. However, selling gold without government permission is illegal in Sudan.

Government official collecting gold from a gold
farmer (witnessed by Sebastian Joseph)

Why Did Germany Colonize Namibia for 106 years?

The history of Namibia has several distinct stages, from being colonized in the late nineteenth century to Namibia's independence on 21 March 1990. Since 1884, Namibia had been a German colony, called German South West Africa. The country's natural resources included diamonds, copper, gold, uranium, lead, tin, zinc, salt, vanadium, fisheries, and wildlife, as well as suspected deposits of oil, coal, and iron ore. Agricultural products include livestock, fish, millet, grapes, and wool. Hitler mined the uranium to make bombs. Is Namibia poor?

Why Did the Netherlands and Great Britain Colonize South Africa for More Than Three Centuries?

And incidentally, why is Great Britain so "great"? Is stealing wealth from other countries "great"?

The two European countries that occupied South Africa were the Netherlands (1652-1795 and 1803-1806) and Great Britain (1795- 1803 and 1806-1961). Although South Africa became a union with its own government of white people in 1910, the country was still regarded as a British colony until 1961. South Africa's natural resources include gold, chromium, platinum, antimony, coal, iron ore, manganese, nickel, phosphates, and tin. What benefits do the Black South Africans receive from these assets? Is South Africa poor?

Why Was Colonization of the Congo Shared by Europeans for More Than a Century?

Colonization of the Congo refers to the European colonization of the Congo region of tropical Africa. By the end of the 19th century, the Congo Basin had been carved up by European colonial powers into the Congo Free State, French Congo, Portuguese Congo, and Belgian Congo. The Belgian Congo was from 1908-1960, the Congo Free State from 1885-1908, the Congo Crisis from 1960-1965, and the Second Congo War from 1998-2003. The country is still at war. Natural resources of the Congo are centered on the mining industry; the country is one of the world's primary producers of cobalt, copper, diamonds, tantalum, tin, and gold. Is the Congo poor?

Why Did Great Britain Colonize Nigeria for More Than a Century?

Britain annexed Lagos in 1861 and established the Oil River Protectorate in 1884. British influence in the Niger area increased gradually during the 19th century, but Britain did not effectively occupy the area until 1885. Apart from petroleum, Nigeria's natural resources include natural gas, tin, iron ore, coal, limestone, niobium, lead, zinc, and arable land. The oil and gas revenues account for about 10 percent of GDP, and export of petroleum products represents around 86 percent of total export revenue. But still today, the majority of Nigerians are poor—why?

Why Have Arabs and Europeans Colonized Kenya for More Than Sixty-Eight Years?

The British Empire established the East Africa Protectorate in 1895. Beginning in 1920, it was known as the Kenya Colony. The independent Republic of Kenya was formed in 1963. It was ruled as a de facto one-party state by the Kenya African National Union (KANU), led by Jomo Kenyatta from 1963-1978. Kenya has different natural resources spread out across the country. Some of these resources include arable land, soda ash, limestone, gemstones, diatomite, zinc, fluorspar, gyp- sum, gas, oil, hydropower, and wildlife. Is Kenya poor?

Why Did Europeans Colonize the Central African Republic for More Than a Century (and Why Is It Still Under Colonization)?

The European invasion of Central African territory began in the late 19th century during the scramble for Africa. Europeans—primarily French, Germans, and Belgians—arrived in the area in 1885. France seized and colonized the Ubangi-Shari territory in 1894. Natural resources of the Central African Republic include gold, diamonds, uranium, and oil. Is this country poor? With those assets, it shouldn't be, and yet the people depend on charity from the United Nations to feed their children. In what way is the United Nations bringing justice to this country? If they want to solve their problems, how long will that take? Despite everything, somehow guns and artillery are always available for civil war. If the country is poor, then who is paying for the weapons?

The cases cited above are just a few examples. There are fifty-five African countries, all rich with different natural resources. But Europe's agenda is to cause Africans to fight one another, so they can sell weapons and loot Africa's assets. If those fifty-five countries could unite instead of fighting one another, then Africa would be wealthy and untouchable.

The time of exploitation must come to an end. The people of Africa must realize their potential and demand that their leaders support the end of colonization dynamics, so that Africa will not be poor anymore. Your mothers and sisters should not be carrying 50kg items on their heads to sell in the streets to make a living.

CHAPTER 10

Child Military in Africa?

When a boy reaches the age of three or four, one of his dreams will be a toy gun. He will enjoy it more if the gun discharges something—light, water, or other harmless things. But what if a boy of nine or ten years old gets an AK47 that shoots real bullets? That boy will want to be a soldier, and no matter what his circumstances are, he will go with the group that lets him shoot that gun. He may not understand the result of that game or the ultimate disaster behind it.

https://www.google.com/search?q=child+girls+military+in+africa

This is happening in Africa—and who supplies these weapons? Colonialists, you say that Africa is poor and you are supplying them with aid because they are poor. But somehow, Africa always has the latest weapons, even if they don't have food to eat or milk for their children. You may see a child soldier carrying the latest gun, but you will also see that his clothing is torn and ragged, hardly covering his body. What is the motivation behind this bloodiest of bloody games?

You can refer to the website mentioned below to see pictures of child labor, soldiers, and slaves to the people who are looting Africa's wealth.

https://www.accord.org.za/conflict-trends/understanding-recruitment- child-soldiers-africa/

Understanding the Recruitment of Child Soldiers in Africa
By Anne-Lynn Dudenhoefer

While it is estimated that about 40% of all child soldiers globally are active on the African continent, scholars appear to evaluate this number in different ways.

The benefits of recruiting child soldiers seem to be concealed when first approaching the topic. Why would any army or military movement rely on the inferior physical power and inexperience of children? Why are children the "weapon of choice" in so many countries?

From Pakistan and Afghanistan, many children are trained by terrorist groups to be become suicide bombers, but they don't know even how to read or write.

A few years ago, a Pakistani journalist reported a quote from police speaking to a terrorist whose penis was covered by a steel plate. The police asked him why, and he said, "After I die in this bomb blast, I will get to heaven, because I am doing this for God. I will get seventy beautiful girls to enjoy, so I need to protect my penis."

Can you imagine this training? There is no holy book that says you go to heaven for killing people. This is only one example. What are African children being told about what they will get if they die as warriors? God only knows.

You might notice, while watching TV news about Africa, that the men and the child soldiers carry the latest weapons, and yet children are hungry and infants do not have milk—their mothers' breasts are dry, and they barely have the strength to stand. These are the types of pictures shown to prove that Africa is a poor country. During the civil war in Somalia in the 1980s, thousands of people died like animals—they died in every way and rotted, and you could see people walking over skeletons without even moving them.

But every day, guns and bullets will be delivered on time. Those of you who transport weapons—do you know their value? An entire village could eat for a month with the money required to supply weapons for a day. The African people must understand that these weapons are not being given to you for protection. All they will do is spoil the economy and steal assets. When you die, your value is less than that of a dog. Just for their own benefit, political leaders are killing their own people.

Most of the African military recruitments happen for American and European countries, especially from the Dominican Republic, the Congo, and neighboring countries. They will be posted directly to Iraq, Libya, Syria, and countries controlled by the United Nations—the places where people wage war through labor contracts with small salaries, on which their families can barely survive. The recruiting country may pay a high wage, but the mediators/contractors consume all the money. Most of the soldiers will never come back home—this is the latest way to enslave Africans.

There are child soldiers all around the world, from Myanmar to Colombia, but more than half of the child soldiers live in Africa. They are children, not soldiers. As part of their recruitment, children are sometimes forced to kill or maim a family member. This breaks the bonds the child has with the community and makes it hard for them to go home. The child soldiers are sent out to do whatever they are told to do. The children could be fighting against terrorist groups, the government, and anything that country's army is fighting against.

The child soldiers aren't always fighting. Child soldiers are boys and girls under the age of eighteen who are part of any kind or regular or irregular armed force or armed group in captivity. The child soldiers are also used as cooks; sometimes they are used as spies, guards, suicide bombers, human shields—and sometimes for sexual purposes. The effects on these children are felt long after their injuries are healed. Children can become desensitized to violence, which damages them for life. Many of these children are not welcome back home because they may have hurt someone in their family. There can also be many years of education lost.

> ➤ Which African families become rich by participating in these military recruitments?
> ➤ For how long can the African people endure these struggles?
> ➤ For how long will the African people be your playthings?
> ➤ Which of the African countries have benefited by going to war with one another?

The only beneficiaries are the arms dealers, who are controlled by European and American manufacturers. There would be no war without the Western world, but then they say they support you and feed you, after looting all your assets?

Now is the time to wake up. The COVID-19 pandemic is the new, eye- opening revolution for Africa to bring back its inner lion with sharp teeth, full of energy to hunt and protect your territory. COVID-19 is already ravaging Europe and America, the countries who colonized you for centuries. It may be the punishment of God, which will save Africa.

The weapons manufacturers and traders must understand that money made on weapons sales may not protect them from COVID-19. The earth has its own policy to control life on earth, and whether you are Black or white, big or small, from the East or West, we all have the same needs, and each of us has only one life.

You can leave a legacy to the next generation that labels you a legendary thief. Your children may be drug addicts, suffering from depression. Why do you want to spoil your children, with your greediness? You may do this because you were poor and you have wanted to be rich and give a better life to your children, but if you don't do this in a good way, then it will be of no use to your children. You can see many examples of this in wealthy families. Or you will see, before you die, that your children will reject you, and you will be filled with regret, wondering, "For whom did I make all this money?"

We have seen rich people, men and women, who travel to India or other countries to spend time at spiritual retreat centers, pouring out millions of dollars hoping to find peace. What good is a madman with money?

Since January 2011, there have been reports of child soldiers in the following countries:

Somalia: national army; state-allied armed groups; armed opposition groups

Sudan: national army; armed opposition groups

Libya: national army and other elements of state security forces; armed opposition groups

Central African Republic: state-allied groups

Cote d'Ivoire: national army/state security forces; state-allied armed groups; armed opposition groups

Democratic Republic of Congo: national army and other elements of state security forces; Congolese and foreign armed opposition groups

Chad: armed opposition groups

Rwanda: military support in armed opposition groups

Uganda: armed opposition groups

Note: All of these countries are rich in natural resources. If you look at the globe, they form a line where the oil supply channel flows. But whose agenda is it to spoil these children and the country? Who sponsors these weapons, being put like toys into children's hands? They are using these children to kill their parents. Those who are in control want these children to remain uneducated and never think of their country.

CHAPTER 11

Is The United Nations Supporting Justice?

In 2017, the United Nations' revenue totaled **US $53.2 billion**. This is the most recent year for which there is financial data; it may or may not be accurate.

A slogan of the United Nations claims:

"BY GIVING PEOPLE THE TOOLS TO LEAD HEALTHY, PRO- DUCTIVE LIVES, WE CAN HELP THEM LIFT THEMSELVES OUT OF POVERTY."

A fisherman needs a pole or a net to catch fish so he and his entire family will not come to beg in front of you.

A farmer needs water, fertilizer, and seeds to farm the land, so he and his entire family will not come to beg in front of you.

A sewing machine is what a tailor needs so he and his entire family will not come to beg in front of you. And so on for other needs....

Why has it not occurred to the United Nations to spend 20% of their budget on activities such as those listed above, to help people support themselves, rather than giving charity? Or does the United Nations need people to stay in poverty so that they can collect donations? Recently you might be seen on Instagram and Facebook, a man asking donation with the flashy tie and coat well dressed and showing the video of Madagascar people are eating insects. My question to you, while you are taking video of those poor people why you don't by food and clothes for them at least. You will never do because you need such people to be shown in the public to collect money. This is the people looting the money from UN fund.

Every year, millions of people find ways to transition out of poverty by adopting new farming techniques, such as solar technology, investing in new business opportunities, or finding new jobs. We know that women and girls have a unique power to reshape societies. When you invest in a woman's health and empowerment, it has a ripple effect, helping families, communities, and countries to achieve long-lasting benefits.

Remember, the refugees from Syria, Libya, Yemen, Palestine, Myanmar, etc. were not beggars—a group of weapons sellers made them poor. They were rich or had a decent life before the war or crisis that drove them from their country. Rather than spending their time asking for donations and begging for food, those refugees would prefer to end the war and go back to their own country so they will not require any more charity from the United Nations. The United Nations must focus more time on ending war and less on advertising for donations.

In this century, can you prove that any "peacekeeping" forces from America, Russia, or Europe have actually supported peace? No—rather, they have bombarded countries with their powerful weapons and killed or injured people, including children. These peacekeeping forces have made people homeless, and they became refugees. After they are made into refugees, the colonialists go in with aid and say they are helping their victims. The world police will keep on bombarding until the government can pay for the weapons. After that, these so-called peacekeeping forces will appoint new rulers and leave, or keep control remotely. Not only are the economies of these countries ruined, and the citizens' previous lives stolen from them—they also become refugees and beggars in front of the world. Current examples include Afghanistan, Iraq, Syria, Libya, the Central African Republic, the Republic of Congo, and many other places around the world where wars are happening. How does peacekeeping equate to selling weapons?

For the past twenty-five years, how many billions of dollars have been spent by the United Nations to bring peace to the Central African Republic and the Republic of Congo? What benefit has been given to the people in these countries? Even today, the majority of the children do not know what school is. We must suspect that the peacekeeping forces are controlled by people who want to sell weapons and support the countries that are looting natural resources.

Iraq's leadership may have made a mistake by invading Kuwait—there was no support of justification for that invasion, we must agree that was the wrong thing the Iraqis did to Kuwait. The peacekeeping force came to Kuwait's rescue, and we must be happy about that. But what happened to Iraq? How many young girls, woman, and mothers were rape victims thanks to the peacekeeping forces' brutality, which included torturing and killing the men? How many buildings, schools, and infrastructure have been destroyed? What mistakes did the Iraqi people make to end up like this? Before the war, the Iraqi people had an excellent quality of life, like many other Middle Eastern countries. But how can you explain what has happened to them now? Which country will be the next victims? God only knows.

What contributions have the peacekeeping forces made to Syria? The majority of the people are scattered over different parts of the world with no infrastructure, no homes, no hospitals, no schools, and more than a hundred thousand people, including children, dead . . . and the killing continues, with Syrians becoming refugees around the world. Syria was the breadbasket for many European and Arab countries, and now Syrian refugees beg for food, from refugee camps. The same thing has happened to many countries controlled by peacekeeping forces, but the forces will remain there until colonialists have drained all the natural resources from the country. How many millions of dollars' worth of weapons are imported to these countries, and how many billions of dollars' worth of assets are looted? The United Nations must be audited to see what is really going on in these countries.

Every time a refugee holds out their hands in front of you, begging for a meal, they remember their old life, in tears.

If the United Nations truly serves a good purpose for countries and their people, then the United Nations must take a different approach to the poor people and refugees around the world, if they really want to bring justice to them or help them.

What is the role of the United Nations in the world?

The UN was established after World War II, with the goal of preventing future wars. The UN is an intergovernmental organization designed to maintain international peace and security, develop friendly relations among nations, achieve international cooperation, and be a center for harmonizing the actions of nations. But now its work is the opposite of those goals.

The UN is headquartered on international territory in New York City. World peace, or peace on earth, is the concept of an ideal state of happiness, freedom, and peace among all people and nations on earth. Since 1945, the United Nations and the five permanent members of its Security Council (China, France, Russia, the United Kingdom, and the United States) have operated with the stated aim to resolve conflicts without declarations of war.

Why have only those five countries controlled the United Nations since 1945? Perhaps when the UN was founded, other countries were not capable of handling the world economic crisis, or maybe other countries were too poor. Now many countries are rich and educated, including but not limited to Asia, the Middle East, Africa, Australia, and many more.

There are 195 countries in the world today. 193 countries are members of the UN, and two are non-member observer states: the Holy See and the State of Palestine. Of the five controlling countries, four of the founders (excluding China) were colonizers of the world under the umbrella of the United Nations. Now is the time that all other countries must think about and revise the policies of the United Nations, if the United Nations is to live up to its name.

A handful of countries in control is not "united nations." At least 100 countries must be given equal rights and powers in the United Nations. All decisions must be made with votes from all of these countries—otherwise, the world will never be peaceful. The game is not different from some countries staging an election for the sake of making a show for the people, although both parties join together and mutually agree, internally, to control the country. The same thing happens in the United Nations when they want to take a decision against a specific country. They join as two groups, left wing and right wing, and the country in question is forced to buy weapons from one of these groups. Why should just a few countries be given the right to control the world? All countries and their people should have equal rights to live peacefully.

What charity has been given from these permanent members, other than war and poverty? They are the manufacturers of weapons supplied to Africa and other countries.

Some of you may think that the present colonizer is China, but this is not correct. Yes, they are colonizers in business—they have colonized other countries through business tactics with powerful leadership, but they have done so without corruption, and not by killing people. China opened the door to other countries to come start businesses with full freedom. Moreover, the biggest countries have moved their manufacturing hubs to China. That was China's plan to bring their people out of poverty, and they have succeeded. In doing so, China has learned all kinds of manufacturing techniques to make their own competing products including their own space station.

We cannot complain about China, the manufacturing plant for the whole world. We must accept that because of China, many companies can afford to buy and use products per their financial capacity. How is an average person, earning less than $50 per month, going to purchase shoes valued at more than $50 in the USA? China is not going into other countries without invitation or permission; rather, their manufacturing and export policies are attracting Africa and other countries. It is not China's fault that other countries are incapable of producing their own products. When you and your country are not capable of producing what you need, you will import goods. China is not stopping any countries from opening manufacturing plants in their own countries; rather, they will consult with and assist you to open your own plant.

Of course, you will need support from other countries, and it is your choice which country will help you. Business is a system that you have to develop—then the system will rule business by itself. China made that system, and therefore China is number one in business. This is because of their intelligence. Jealousy will not stop them. China made their future plans for a hundred years in the future, not like other countries' plans for one to five years.

Speaking of the construction sector—China and Turkey are leaders in construction in Africa and the Middle East. Is this China and Turkey's fault?

It is not their fault, because their technology is superior to yours when it comes to constructing roads, buildings, or stadiums.

It is not their fault, because some of your leaders are corrupt and do not value you. With one project, you can see some of the leaders' lifestyles suddenly changing.

It is not their fault, because contracting companies within your countries are not ready to respond to the challenge or take on government policies.

It is not their fault—it is the fault of educated people, with engineering degrees and PhD's who hide when the government decides to give projects to other countries. Even if your country is not capable of handling the project, you can ask for a portion of the job to be given to local contracting companies, with local engineers.

There can be no sentimentality in business. Business must consider only the bottom line. Business people will do their best to get contracts by taking every opportunity to get business and make a profit. You cannot expect charity from business people while they are doing business. Yes, they may be generous after they make their profit, but charity and sentiment cannot be mixed with business. If they are mixed together, businesses fail.

Any form of trespass or interruption from other countries must be prevented. Some countries' leaders kneel in front of China for help without checking their credentials and assets from their own country— again, it is not China's fault. It is the responsibility of each country to protect themselves. The leaders are bowing down in front of other countries; and it is for the benefit of the leader, not for the benefit of the country. You may note that recently, China's military has come into Africa—subsequently, America and European countries are trying to get their military there as well, to get their share. The end result will be that those countries will be destroyed just like the Middle Eastern countries including Iraq, Syria, Libya, Yemen, Egypt, etc. Again, I remind you that no country finds war to be financially beneficial. It only destroys the country's economy and the country itself, while killing citizens.

Let's look again at the four permanent governing members of the United Nations who have been colonialists around the world for centuries, especially in Africa and Asia. These are the countries producing weapons. In one hand they bring peace, and in the other hand they carry weapons? What kind of peacemaking is this? If the goal of the United Nations is to prevent war and protect human life, then why are children in Africa carrying the latest in weapons technology, as if these weapons are toys? Are these boys carrying toy guns? Are they getting guns free from the manufacturers? Who are the sponsors of these weapons? Why are the United Nations peacekeeping forces failing to see this?

https://www.google.com/search?q=african+children+carrying+guns+and+ weapon&tbm

Are weapons being put in the hands of children without the manufacturers' knowledge? We do not see children carrying weapons in where there are no natural resources such as oil, gold, diamonds, uranium, etc. During the World Wars, the raw material to make atom bombs, uranium, was mined from African countries by Germany, France, the United States, Great Britain, and so on. The United Nations can take a survey about the country of origin of the weapons currently sold and used around Africa. None of the African countries are making these weapons; the most they do is assemble a few small guns. What is the point of origin of these weapons flowing into Africa, and if Africa is poor, then who is paying for these weapons? Of course, the manufacturers are not supplying anything to Africa for free.

Is this called peacekeeping in Africa? Are these weapons made in Africa? By looking at the people, you can see that they don't have proper clothing to wear or good food to eat, and yet they carry valuable weapons.

Peace is a concept of societal friendship and harmony in the absence of hostility and violence. In a social sense, peace is commonly used to mean a lack of conflict (such as war) and freedom from fear of violence between individuals or groups. Therefore, I would like to know why the United Nations has been unable to prevent the violence and war in many African and Middle Eastern countries.

We have not seen the following issues resolved by the United Nations. Without a doubt, we can say that this is because the United Nations has put emphasis on protecting Black and white colonialists in their destruction of the countries' economies and their suppression of the citizens, who are afraid to leave their homes and demand their rights. Because if they come out, they will see colonialists looting the natural resources and assets that rightfully belong to them.

- For many years, there have been civil wars and political massacres. How many of these have been truly resolved with the help of the United Nations?
- For how many years have people died, lost their fathers, mothers, children, and loved ones in conflicts in Israel/Palestine, Iran, Iraq, Yemen, Syria, Libya, the Democratic Republic of Congo, Sudan, Egypt, the Central African Republic, Rohingya, Myanmar, and more? Did the United Nations solve any of these issues?
- How many people have fled for their lives, escaping their home country only to end up as refugees?
- Would any of the countries that govern the UN like to have a war in their own country?
- Does any country really want to beg for charity from the UN?
- In whose interest is it to continue the war or crisis?
- Which are the main countries in control of the United Nations?

It is well known by everyone that the countries with the most refugees are rich in one or more natural resources, such as oil, gas, gold, diamonds, precious metals, minerals, gemstones, etc.

The United Nations must ask these refugees which option they prefer:

#1: For the UN to stop the war or political crisis in their country, so they can return home

#2: For the UN to give them aid

I don't think anyone would choose the second option.

The ongoing wars and political crises benefit only weapons manufacturers, and less than 5% of politicians and people in business.

The time has come to stop this dirty game, because technology is at everyone's fingertips via mobile phone, even if they are poor refugees. If the United Nations truly wants to do good to countries and their people, then it is time to take a different approach, because none of them want to continue suffering.

Sometimes we may wonder why God seems to support only white people. If God Loves Black people, why has He allowed Africa and its people to suffer under slavery and poverty for more than seven centuries? How long must a person pray before God hears? Why is God not answering these prayers?

But now God is going to hear Africa's prayer, as signified by the new movement in the United States, the Black revolution against racism and white colonialism. This will spread across the world, especially to Europe, and it is a good start against White Supremacy. Similarly, the African people, especially the younger generation and the students, must unite and gather together to cleanse the government of bad leadership. Always remember that you are not at the mercy of political leaders— rather, they are at your mercy. You give them power. Enough is enough, and you must tap into your full energy and rise from the flames like the phoenix.

The Black diaspora living in the USA, Europe, and other parts of the world are the children of Africa.

- Your DNA is in Africa. You may have citizenship or a green card, but you should not forget that your forefathers arrived as slaves.
- Centuries later, some leaders shed blood and sacrificed their lives to be free from slavery.
- It is your duty to support the prosperity and security of Mother Africa.
- It is your responsibility to set your mother free.
- The souls of your forefathers who fought for freedom will not be at peace if you do not return Africa to her wealth.
- Africa's land is so fertile that with a small investment, your investment can yield a tenfold income.
- You may make a good living now, but expenses are also high. In effect, you are not making a profit, and you remain second-class citizens.
- But if you make the same effort in Africa that you are making in another country, you will become wealthy while returning justice to your homeland.

For more than 600 years, white colonialists have continuously enslaved and murdered the black community through White Supremacy. How long will you allow this to go on? So far, the Black community has not colonized or murdered the white community. If Black people started to behave the way white people have behaved for centuries, there would be worldwide disaster. It is better that white colonialists stop their racist activities.

Is it time to think of a different United Nations?

Your time must start now.

To My People in Africa

"Plants that need watering will never be big trees. Large trees are the plants that can find water with their own roots." – Aristotle, Greek Philosopher

The children of Africa must face the truth that **YOUR RESOURCES ALONE ARE NOT ENOUGH; YOU MUST WORK TOGETHER TO CHANGE PUBLIC POLICIES, ATTITUDES, AND BEHAV- IORS TO CHANGE LIVES, ESPECIALLY TO IMPROVE THE LIVES OF POOR PEOPLE AND TO STABILIZE AFRICA'S ECONOMY.**

It is not your fault if you are born poor, but if you die poor, that is your fault, and only your fault.

No prophets who came before us said that people should die poor. They spoke only of doing well in this world, living well, and being comfortable in the Hereafter. The prophets' words speak of human good, irrespective of race, caste, or creed. God created Satan in the same way, and those devils are still in our midst, in many forms and roles. It is our duty to identify the devils around us, and it is the duty of each of you to find and eliminate those devils. God has reserved eternal fire for such devils and their offspring—their time is near. The money they have stolen is their grave, and the graves of the generations to come.

What our country needs is knowledge and intelligence, more than man- power or military power. Every African leader should help the people of their own country not to depend on arms dealers. ***Once you stop fighting, they will come to beg from you, because you are the kings and queens of Africa.*** The dirty animals who sell weapons should beware.

Every African leader must think about why we need weapons, and why we feel the need to fight with neighboring countries. How many countries are better off because of war? It is not in the best interest of Africa or its people to fight each other—it is in the interest of the other countries who attacked, colonized, and enslaved you for many centuries, who caused you to be poor so that they could exploit your precious natural resources. To this day, those who colonized Africa are still ruling through the power of leaders they have selected. Therefore, Africa is the same—poor and underdeveloped. How many Black Africans are well off and have a good job in Europe, Africa, or some of the Middle Eastern countries? You can see that many of them work menial jobs— housekeepers, manual labor, etc.—despite being educated. It is time for Africans to unite to fulfill your dreams.

It is noteworthy that to this day, in India, the Middle East, and Africa, when a white person enters a government office, the officials stand up and serve them. But when a Black person or a poor person comes in for the same purpose, the same employees treat them disrespectfully, even if the person is old enough to be the employee's parent. Why does it matter to the employee if the person is Black, white, rich, or poor? And how can you tell just from looking at someone whether they are rich or poor? For all you know, the person may be ten times wealthier than you are, but they stand patiently in front of you because the country's law demands that they do so. It isn't like this everywhere—in other countries, everyone pays the same fee and gets the same service. Of course, even in the countries mentioned, there are some government officers and employees who are very nice and treat everyone equally . . . it just isn't as common.

To overcome this, African people must get out of the habit of thinking of yourselves as Black and poor. This inferiority complex keeps you down, and you must sharpen your thinking like the tiger's teeth. Who has permission to control you or tell you where you can go and whom you can speak to, based only on race or color? White, black, brown, red—these are only skin colors. Do not accept this nonsense anymore. The white people came to you originally as beggars, and you knelt before them because you thought they were kind and beautiful. But because you bent your head and back to them, they climbed on top of you and have stayed there ever since.

"A dream is not what you see in sleep—a dream is the thing that doesn't let you sleep." –Dr. APJ Abdul Kalam, former President of India

Yes, the time has come for you to dream—dream of things that you believe will happen. First and foremost, you need confidence that your dreams can become reality. There are objects in your house—did they ask for permission to be there? You are an African, and Africa is your home. You have the right to dream, and to own your place in your homeland.

It is you who have chosen your leaders. As the saying goes, **"The mother is more concerned about the crying baby."** In the same way, you must cry louder and louder until your problems are resolved. As Martin Luther King Jr. said during the Civil Rights movement in the United States, **"If you can't fly then run; if you can't run then walk; if you can't walk then crawl to reach your destination."** Then and only then will your country's leaders listen to you. Why have you forgotten to ask for what you need? This attitude has to change—it is your mindset that hinders your success and ambition. **"Even death cannot defeat you if your dreams are strong."** Yes, the forefathers who fought for freedom from white colonialism will always be remembered. But the problem is that in the current generation, that brave and necessary work is not being emulated. Later generations wrote the stories of those inspiring ancestors, put the books in libraries, and made statues for the birds to sit on.

Some of the young people in Africa today don't even know who these men are who fought so hard to be free of colonialism. It is the elders' responsibility to convey these stories to the younger generation so that we may see their like again. Here are some of their names: Martin Luther King Jr (USA); Nelson Mandela (South Africa); Haile Selassie (Ethiopia); Kenneth Kaunda (Zambia); Kwame Nkrumah (Ghana); Thomas Sankara (Burkina Faso); Ahmadou Ahidjo (Cameroon); Sylvanus Olympio (Togo); Ruben Um Nyobè (Cameroon); Philibert Tsiranana (Madagascar); Mohammed Abdullah Hassan (Somalia); Joseph Kasa-Vubu (Congo); Ahmed Sékou Touré (Guinea); Léopold Sédar Senghor (Senegal); Nnamdi Azikiwe (Nigeria).

If your dreams are real, then the **Law of Attraction** works. If your thoughts are true, then God will open the way for you. You must believe the truth in the saying that **"God never closes one door without opening at least two other doors. You do not see the two new doors because you are crying behind the door that closed."** If you spend your time asking, "O God, why did You do this to me?" then you will never see what God has given to you. When God closes a door, you must be happy; that door was closed because it wasn't right for you. There may be some mistakes on the other side of that door that you are not yet aware of—so your job is to find your mistake, learn from it, and ask God to show you the other, better doors that He has opened for you.

Everything around you that you see, touch, use, etc. was somebody's dream before it became reality.

The Secret is a best-selling 2006 self-help book by **Rhonda Byrne**, based on the earlier film of the same name. It is based on the theory of the Law of Attraction, which claims that thoughts can change a person's life directly. The book has sold 30 million copies worldwide and has been translated into fifty languages. There are also many other books available to inspire you regarding the Law of Attraction.

Yes, the Law of Attraction works—if you wish for it, you will have it.

"Seeds that grow only by rain
Some of the soil does not come to mind
The only thing that matters are love
Inside the spirit." –Rafeeq Ahmed, Indian Poet

The words quoted above are lyrics the poet wrote for a romantic movie, but these words can be used in your own life to make you better.

There are many ways to improve your life, even if you are not getting much support from your government. Maybe the government will have other priorities than your needs, to protect the country. When there are obstacles in your life, try to rise like the phoenix from ancient Greek folklore, the long-lived bird that cyclically regenerates or is born again. Associated with the sun, a phoenix is resurrected by rising from the ashes of its predecessor.

If you live as if you have lost everything in life right now, then what are you waiting for? This is the time when you must make the decision to do or die. **"It is better to live for no good than to die for any good."** Then at least the generation after you will have a better future. Those who make such sacrifices are the people we still remember today. In order to think in these terms, you must love yourself first. Your spirit must come out from within, like an eagle. When the eagle's wings get too heavy, it goes off by itself and pulls out its own feathers. Can you imagine how painful that must be? But the eagle knows that only through this pain will new feathers grow, allowing it to fly high again. You must be willing to endure pain before you can take flight. To do this requires intelligence and understanding, rather than brute strength.

There will be nothing in the world that can stop you, if you join together with like-minded people.

You can pool your small savings and start a business—it can be a small agricultural business if you are from a farming background. This is the only area in which no government will interrupt your work; rather, they will support you, because everyone wants to eat. Start a small work- shop—steel or aluminum fabrication, engine repair, etc. What are you good at? Start a tailoring business if you know how to sew. That's how your dream comes true—start small and grow big.

## CHAPTER 13

How Do I Start a Business? I Don't Know How!

It's not your fault that you are not an entrepreneur, because our educational system has a structure focused on getting a degree to get a good job and become an employee.

Rich Dad, Poor Dad and **Rich Dad's Cash Flow Quadrant**: These two books are guides to financial freedom. The follow-up book reveals why some people work less, earn more, pay less in taxes, and feel more financially secure than others. These books will help you to break free from working for others and find your way as a business person or entrepreneur.

Rich Dad, Poor Dad is a 1997 bestseller by Robert Kiyosaki and Sharon Lechter. It advocates the importance of financial literacy, financial independence, and building wealth through investing in assets, etc.

No one becomes successful or rich only by reading books and motivational stories. You must put in effort and have a vision or dream, and you must hope to achieve something in life. You must be wholeheartedly committed to making your dream a reality, and then the Law of Attraction will work for you.

There is nothing wrong with being an employee, but not many people become rich or financially independent that way. Your salary will be limited, and based on your salary, you will become part of a systemic structure designed to maintain your family peacefully without disturbing anyone. But sometimes you may encounter unexpected financial problems. Yes, you can borrow money from your friends or from the bank, but what if emergencies keep happening? This is when many people are forced to surrender their ethics and values and think of some less-honest ways to get money quickly. This is called corruption, and it is common among government employees and political leaders around the world. Unfortunately, many leaders in Africa and India fall into this category.

Your salary will not always cover you and your family's needs, so you must build an alternative solution while you are on the job.

How?

No one becomes rich without taking risks.

You can start a business or service based on something you know well or have experience with, or you can partner with someone you trust. It can be with your investment alone or with someone else, depending on the savings you have accumulated. It can be your idea or your partner's idea. That is how you leverage your time. God has given only twenty-four hours a day to each human being. The formula for the average person is eight hours of work, eight hours of sleep, eight hours for other duties and personal time. This may not be applicable for those who wish to move from employment to entrepreneurship. You have to sacrifice a few of your personal hours to get ahead.

A great deal of thought, research, and planning must go into a successful business. Do not jump in immediately without having a vision plan for three to five years. You must observe and listen to successful entrepreneurs, and you can also learn from those who have failed in business, so you can learn from their mistakes.

Let me share an example, a businessman in the Middle East, Europe, and India who is now expanding to other continents and will soon be active in Africa. His Excellency DR. M. A. Yusuff Ali (full name Yusuff

Ali Musaliam Veettil Abdul Kader) is a UAE-based Indian billionaire businessman. He is the founder, chairman, and managing director of LULU Group International that owns the LULU Hypermarket chain worldwide and LULU International with more over 145 shopping malls. While I am writing this book, LULU groups will be adding (their 146th) another mall under construction.

He came to the Middle East and worked as a regular employee, but now he is one of the richest businessmen in the world. His company was founded in the year 2000, and as of March 2020, his revenue was 7.4 billion USD. More than 57,000 people work directly with LULU Group, and others indirectly. He supports many charitable organizations and he donates to the Indian government. Of course, it hasn't been easy, and he did not succeed overnight.

In an interview, Yousuff gave advice to owners of small and medium- sized businesses. When his first supermarket business became successful, after struggles and challenges, many people advised him to immediately open a second one. But he waited until he had ample capital to open four more supermarkets. **"This is called vision and dreams with dedication and patience."**

You may ask: **"How can I start an agricultural business? I am not a farmer, and I don't have land."**

But it is possible, if you have a dream, and a passion to start your own small farm or agricultural business.

The leader is the one who chooses the right people for each job and works with them.

It is not necessary for you to have vast technical knowledge about agriculture; nor must you have your own land. You might have noticed, if you work for an employer, that the person you work for does not know how to do your specific job. He may not even come in to the office where you work, if it is a large business. He has purchased eight or ten hours of your time every day, and in return, you are paid a salary. You have no right to that eight or ten hours, after you sign a contract with him. Unfortunately, you have become like a loyal dog—the only difference is that you don't have a collar and leash. The dog is better off; it doesn't have to put up with the tension and pressure that you're under as an employee. But like a dog, you come and go at your boss's bidding, and you will always fear him more than you respect him. During the hours that you are on duty, you can't even see your spouse without permission—I mean it! You can't see your own spouse!

Look into your heart and ask yourself:

- Do you really like your boss?
- If you are a boss, ask yourself whether you really want your son or daughter to work as a salaried employee. I am sure that 90 percent of you will answer "no."
- Does this sound to you like a form of legal slavery?
- Your boss may not be as well qualified as you are, or he may not even have graduated with the same degrees you have, even though you must call him "sir"! But you can't afford these thoughts, because you have no other choice.
- Have you ever thought about sleeping another two hours without setting an alarm in the morning?
- Wouldn't you like to play with your children for a week without having to report for duty?
- Have you ever cursed traffic during work hours?
- Have you ever thought of turning off your mobile phone to get away from your job during work hours?

The dog's leash may be one or two meters long, but since you carry your mobile phone in your hand, no matter how far away you are from your boss, he can pull you back to him while you are on duty.

Remember, medical science has proven that the majority of heart attacks are reported on Sunday nights. Because Monday, you must go back to work.

You might have heard the story of the bird in a cage.

When the owner of the bird provides food and water on time, the bird will be happy. It will sing and play. It may lie on its back and bite its wings, and it can walk two steps forward and two steps back—it is protected from other animals by the cage and by its owner. But despite all these advantages, the bird loses one thing: freedom. The longer the bird is in the cage, it may forget how to fly.

One day, a man decided to free his pet bird. He put his hand inside the cage to release the bird, but it was afraid and tried to get away. He continued to attempt to catch the bird, but the bird was still afraid. Somehow he caught the bird and allowed it to fly away, but the bird came back to the cage. This time, the man took the bird and put it in a tree. Now the bird didn't know what to do—it was afraid to go back to the cage, but it looked around in trepidation and fear. Then it saw other birds like him, flying and playing freely, mating with their partners. The bird realized that there was more to life than his cage, and he returned to his instincts.

When you open a business of your own, no matter how big or small it is, you are now the boss. When you own a business, you don't need to set an alarm. You can enjoy sitting at a street café at 10:00 a.m. wearing shorts and a t-shirt, watching the traffic go by, eating breakfast with your partner and enjoying the weather. After that, you can fly, like the bird in the story, to different countries with your family to enjoy a vacation. Don't you think that your family would like to travel to Disneyland or the African jungle or anywhere else in the world that calls to them? To achieve those dreams, you must change yourself first. You must have a real dream and work toward it. It is not easy, and it requires your total dedication and sacrifice to get started.

If you are ready to invest or you have a group of investors, then it is easy to find farmers who have land, but who do not have money to buy water pumps or other equipment—they need help with the initial investment. You can approach them and make an agreement to partner with the farmer, or you can approach the farmer with your investment proposal, and most governments will be happy to assist you, because this will produce food for the country and jobs for people. In other words, you are being charitable to bring a better life to the farmers.

Fortunately, most of Africa is blessed with fertile land. You can grow organic fruits and vegetables and charge twice what conventionally grown produce costs, because you don't need to fertilize most of the land. The reason is that Africa is the only continent that still has unpolluted soil. For that reason, Europe and the Middle East prefer vegetables and fruits from Africa. (by the way, most of the time this flight might be carrying the looted gold or diamond as well, this is what the local people says) You just need to bring water to your land, and once you do that, you can think of adding other products. For example, since you will have water, you can produce animal feed on the same land, for your own animals, and farm sheep and cattle. The sheep and cattle will also produce natural fertilizer for your fam. Within a year, your flock of sheep will double in number. In the second year, their reproduction will be exponential, if you take good care of them.

If you have a large pond, you can propagate fish on your farm, an endeavor which will give you a return in a year's time. You can think of adding ducks and hens, to produce eggs and meat. And then you can think of exporting your products, first locally, and then to other parts of the world. Once your farm is self-sustaining, you can manage it without living there . . . but you can visit with your family and the children can play on the farm with the animals, in the fresh air. Wouldn't that be lovely for you and your family?

This dream all depends on your hard work, your dedication, and your ideas. Again, remember that without hard work, nobody can achieve their dreams or goals.

A child may fall several times while growing up, but that child keeps trying, with a smile on their face, until they succeed. You must copy the attitude of that child when you are starting a business for the first time.

What if you don't have enough money to start a business?

Money isn't actual property—it is a form of license from the government, something to keep that represents property and power.

Unfortunately, some people know how to use money, and others don't. Some hide their money in the bank or elsewhere, thinking that it belongs to them. But no one brought money with them when they were born, and nobody will take it with them when they die.

You don't need your own money, in order to start a business. You can borrow from any source, or you can sell your ideas and technical knowledge to partner with the business you are entering into. Starting a small business does not require big money. The richest people in the world never had enough money to start their own business. But they had technical knowledge and ideas that made them business tycoons.

Here are some examples—you can research their lives to learn more about how they became tycoons.

Dhirubhai Ambani was a regular employee who became an Indian business tycoon; he is the founder of Reliance Industries. Ambani took Reliance public in 1977 and was worth $26.5 billion at his death on 6 July 2002. Later, all of his businesses were inherited by his children. His son, Mukesh Dhirubhai Ambani, is an Indian billionaire business magnate with a net worth of over 52 billion. He is now the chairman, managing director, and largest shareholder of Reliance Industries Ltd., a Fortune Global 500 company and India's most valuable company by market value. As of April 2020, Mukesh Ambani is one of the richest man in Asia.

William Henry Gates III is an American business magnate, software developer, investor, and philanthropist. He is best known as the co-founder of Microsoft Corporation. As of May 2020, his net worth was US $105.6 billion.

Steven Paul Jobs was an American business magnate, industrial designer, investor, and media proprietor, the founder of Apple. As of September 2011, his net worth was US $7 billion.

Do you still believe that you have no money? Then you should write a book explaining that you cannot start a business because you have no money. If the book is a success, you can use the royalties to start your own business!

## CHAPTER 14

Dream, Dream, Dream!

You've heard many times that you should dream and keep dreaming. But is it practical?

Read this slowly:

GODISNOWHERE
God is nowhere?
or
God is now here?

It depends on how you take it in your mind. This thought-provoking message came to me via WhatsApp from my big brother in Nigeria, Mr. Dele Momo.

When you're discouraged, a beautiful mantra is: **"Life depends on our attitude."**

This is true, but if you do nothing but dream, you will never accomplish anything. You have to put in effort, and your dreams may be difficult to achieve. Your dream may be a pop-up message from God while you are sleeping, traveling, sharing stories of successful people within your community or around the world—and not everyone may hear your message. Or it can be like a holy book that you take with you to read; if you are really seeking something before you read the holy book, you may get what you are looking for. Otherwise, you will not see the book's relevance to your life.

As the author of this book, I must share some of my experiences regarding how I have achieved my dreams, which I thought to be impossible all my life. But God could not refuse my unquenchable desire.

I am Sebastian Joseph, an Indian from the State of Kerala, known as "God's Own Country," meaning an area, region, or place supposedly favored by God. Kerala, a state on India's tropical Malabar Coast, has nearly 600km of shoreline on the Arabian Sea. This is the first place where colonialists landed in India. It is known for its palm-lined beached and backwaters, and a network of canals. Inland are the Western Ghats, mountains whose slopes support tea, coffee, and spice plantations as well as wildlife. National like Eravikulam and Periyar, plus Wayanad and other sanctuaries, are home to elephants, langur monkeys, and tigers. It looks like some places in Africa, such as Kenya, or Zanzibar in Tanzania.

I was born into a very poor family with a total of ten children. I have nine siblings: five elder brothers, three elder sisters, and one younger sister. My mother knows only how to love, along with my father, who hides all of life's little hardships and laughs happily in front of others.

I was a dreamer at an early age—both the dream and the desire to see it come true were very intense. One of my biggest dreams was to have three meals a day. There was a glass display case at a tea shop in front of my house, which displayed food that I was craving. My brother and sister and I would count what was going inside the display case, but when the time came to go to school, we stopped counting and went on with an empty stomach, because we had no money to buy the food. This happened most days.

One day in my biology class, I fell asleep. The teacher shouted at me, "Did you overeat? Is that why you are sleepy?" I smiled and apologized. Yes, science tells us that when a person overeats, they may become sleepy. But the teacher didn't know that my stomach was empty.

Let me share one more story. We had two hens at our house, and most days, we would get two eggs from the hen. My sisters collected and sold the eggs to buy household supplies; getting to eat a whole egg was a dream for me at that time. One day when I was in primary school, 2nd standard, during the exams we had to buy our own paper. There was no money in the house, so my sister gave me two eggs and told me to sell them to the neighbor so I could buy my paper. My sister told me to be careful with the eggs. In trying to keep the eggs safe, I pressed them together too hard and they broke. I was afraid to go back home. I went to the neighbor's house in tears, carrying the broken eggs. The neighbor, a kind woman, understood my innocence and gave me not only the money but also breakfast. I will always cherish the memory of that neighbor.

My mother always added the extra ingredient of love to the food she made. Even though there wasn't much to eat, we all were strong and healthy, and I am sure it is because of the Vitamin L (Love) my mother added to our food. After meals, our house was full of joy and singing. The whole family, including my parents, loved to sing, though we were not trained singers. This caused jealousy even among mothers who could afford to feed their children every day. When I sat down to eat, my elder sisters would stay near me with a handheld fan, because we did not have electricity in the house. Since I was the youngest boy, I had the privilege of love from all my brothers and sisters. My sisters would give me their food without hesitation and go to bed hungry. From a very young age, I knew what love was.

In those difficult times, job opportunities were very rare in my home town, and therefore my brothers tried everything they could to help support my parents. Similarly, I started earning money at the age of ten, by selling peanuts in the street. When I reached tenth grade in school, I was earning enough to pay my school fees and have a little pocket money, without asking my parents. **This was when my first dream came true—to have three meals a day.**

Our house was a hut; it leaked in rainy weather, and a shower of rain bathed us at night during the rainy season. We did not have a good blanket to cover us. Still I remember my mother, during the rainy season, like a hen covering her chicks with her wings, holding me and my younger sister at night.

At the age of twenty, I reached the wonderful country of Qatar, where I began working to support my family. This great country has given so much to me and to my family. My brothers and I built a better house for my parents. **This was my second dream—a better home, to dry my mother's tears and protect my sisters.** This was followed by the marriages of my brothers and sisters, and each of them now own one or more homes. **My fourth and fifth dreams were now reality.**

At last, God has given me my beautiful wife, Patricia, who is the foundation of my success. She has never complained, and she has always given me strength, through her love, despite my ups and downs in business. We are blessed with three lovely boys—Aby, Seby, and Jabin.

I had the chance to attend different kinds of motivational training and seminars that showed me how to dream and make those drams a reality. I decided to make my dream of a duplex villa into reality. **I have now achieved my sixth biggest dream.** It is a blessing from God, and now I am the only person in my region to have three duplex villas.

I have started my own business (think of it—I've gone from selling peanuts to working with PC's!). My first business was an IT solutions company in Qatar (www.itsqatar.net) and with my partners, I started a 3-star hotel, La-Castle Hotel (www.lacastlehotel.qa). But I didn't stop there. I started an agricultural business, growing onions, vegetables, and sheep in Sudan, with my Sudanese partner. It is a fully solar-powered farm, and we also supply solar-powered pumps to farmers in Sudan. If they cannot afford to buy a pump, we support them with an interest free loan to help develop their farms. This was part of my dream to give back through charity, and in doing that, **I have achieved my seventh dream.**

I represent a multinational exploration company, GeoResonance Company Limited, Australia and Singapore (www.georesonance. com) as the marketing manager for the Middle East and Africa. The Middle East office is in Qatar, and you can reach me at (sebastian@ georesonance. co).

I have traveled around the world, to thirty-five countries so far, and I have met ambassadors, ministers, and presidents of African countries. **I have achieved my eighth dream, which was to travel around the world.**

So far, I have achieved fifteen of my dreams. My dream list is large— it never ends. How many dreams can you write down?

Dreams do not come true in a day or two, or even in a few weeks. I am now fifty-two years old, and it took thirty-two years to achieve most of my dreams. But dreams come to you in life; most of the time they will come without your permission, and when they come, you should write them down in your diary.

You were born because your existence was your father and mother's dream. You may complete a job or educational training, you may marry a wonderful partner, you may be using a high-end mobile phone . . . all of those things are your dreams.

If you wish for it, you can definitely have it, but you must put in effort to achieve it.

Martin Luther King Jr. was a Black American, a Christian minister and activist who became the most visible spokesperson and leader in the Civil Rights movement, from 1955 until his assassination in 1968. He played a key role in the American Civil Rights movement, and his dream was a country free of racism, white colonialism, and slavery for Black Americans and for the remaining slaves around the world. His dream came true a few years after his assassination.

The real Lion of Africa, Nelson Rolihlahla Mandela, was a South African anti-apartheid revolutionary, political leader, and philanthropist who served as President of South Africa from 1994 to 1999. He was the country's first Black head of state and the first elected in a fully representative democratic election. He sacrificed his entire life, spending twenty-seven years in jail, to achieve one of his greatest dreams—to win freedom for Black people.

Mahatma Gandhi was an Indian lawyer, anti-colonial nationalist, and political ethicist, who employed nonviolent resistance to lead the successful campaign for India's independence from British Rule, and in turn inspire movements for civil rights and freedom across the world. The dream came true for the people of India.

WHAT ARE YOU WAITING FOR? What is stopping you from dreaming?

How to Develop Africa

The countries listed below are blessed with oil reserves or with metals and gemstones such as gold, diamonds, copper, etc. Each country has more than one natural resource. Some countries make some limited use of their resources, and others do not; some countries' assets are looted and exploited by colonialists.

Liberia, Ivory Coast, Ghana, Nigeria, Cameroon, the Central African Republic, the Democratic Republic of Congo, Sudan, Ethiopia, Somalia, Tanzania, Uganda, Kenya, Burundi, Bali, Botswana, Senegal, Djibouti, and across the Red Sea into Arab countries— these are the world's main sources of gold and diamonds. But the citizens of the countries with this wealth do not benefit from it.

These areas are also known for their poverty, but in reality, these countries have extensive natural reserves, and people are sleeping on top of gold mines without looking into them—or certain special-interest groups are not allowing them to use their own resources. So instead, they receive aid from the United Nations and other charitable organizations. Are these groups really helping these countries, or are they deliberately killing them?

I met the vice president and minerals minister of an African country who told me, "We know we have reserves, but we have no money to explore and mine."

Other African countries should look to Botswana as a role model, under the leadership of Sir Seretse Khama. Upon gaining independence from Britain in 1966, Botswana was the second-poorest country in the world. It was a tiny country with only 12 kilometers of roads, no hospitals, and no colleges. Among the total population, it had only twenty-two people with university degrees and fewer than 100 people who had graduated from high school. Cattle feed and farming were the only sources of income. But only five decades later, Botswana is one of the richest countries in Africa.

Under the leadership of Sir Seretse Khama, Botswana was ranked as a non-corrupt multi-party democratic country (holding a position near South Korea, Italy, and China for non-corruption). Today, Botswana is one of the largest diamond producers in the world, and a top-ranked exporter of beef and copper.

The president's long-range vision led the country from rags to riches. The president believed in focusing on the potential of the country's natural reserves to benefit the people, rather than focusing on military power. Botswana is ranked as the fastest-growing economy in the world, with the support of the least-corrupt civil servants in the country. Botswana has successfully invested in the public sector with basic infrastructure, free hospital facilities, free education, subsidies for agriculture and cattle farming, etc. After developing the country, then they formed a military defense system to protect the country.

The new leader in Tanzania

John Pombe Magufuli is a Tanzanian politician and the fifth President of Tanzania, in office since 2015. He is also the chairman of the Southern African Development Community. He is another fearless visionary, who is trying, along with his team, to stabilize and increase the Tanzanian economy. A notable quote from him: "I tell you, my Tanzanian brothers and sisters, there is no grandfather, uncle, or aunt who will come to defend or help us. They will come only to tell you about family planning, and why God said—Go forth, and multiply. They [the white colonialist] are not happy because I am telling you the truth. Tanzania is the richest country. We have gold, tanzanite, diamonds, fertile land, and so on. Once you have industries, you create jobs and employment for young people. We killed Tanzanian jobs and employment. We killed the fruit industry and became importers. We import even tomatoes. When the tomatoes are grown, they grow everywhere in the country, and yet we continued to celebrate. We farm cotton, and then we sell raw cotton—why? They make the clothes, they wear them, and then donate second-hand clothes back to us. Everything we export is raw materials. If you export raw materials, you have created jobs for them. That's why we must decide to start with the industries, and our policies began to change to support industry. Today we have made changes, but we need to have enough electric power at a low cost. If you have high-cost electric power, you cannot compete with other countries that have low-cost electric power. You cannot have cheap electricity for rent. That's why we decided to construct Nyerere Hydroelectric Power. If the dam starts producing electricity, the price of electricity will go down, and our industries will get enough electricity. Our people will have jobs and employment, and our economy will grow."

Paul Kagame is a Rwandan politician and former military leader. He is the fourth and current President of Rwanda, having taken office when his predecessor, Pasteur Bizimungu, resigned. He has said, "This is un- doubted a difficult period for our region and the entire world. We are working to minimize the economic hardship on our citizens while protecting their health. But this will be more effective, as stated by Your Excellency's, if we act in concert with one another. So long as any member of our community is vulnerable, we are all at risk. Therefore, we must work very closely together in the months ahead, to face this challenge as a community of partners."

President Paul Kagame built Rwanda, passing all the hurdles and surviving a bombardment of objections from both white and Black colonialists in the country. Rwanda has the fastest-growing economy in Africa and is among the fastest-growing in the world, with a 7 to 8% increase. This is also the only president who has given equal representation to women in the cabinet. Women make up 62 percent of

Rwanda's national legislature—far more, proportionally, than any other country. The country's most notable conflict—the 1994 genocide—paved the way for gender equality.

These examples show the first step required of all the countries in Africa. Since your economy is poor, you must focus first on the natural reserves available in your country to produce what your country needs, and then export the rest. When you are poor, no thief will come to your home to steal from you and kill you, so you don't need weapons to protect your country. You must instead protect the people's food, education, and healthcare system. Then the people of your country will protect your country, and they will not think of corruption.

The best fertilizer for the farm is to support the farmers feed—then he will take good care of your farm.

This solution is suitable for countries who really want to grow. A country doesn't need a big investment in order to develop. The African diaspora around the world can support African development. You can found an African shareholding company strategy, where the diaspora can invest—it can be started for as little as $1000, and each person can contribute depending on their capacity. Each African will fund natural resource exploration and mining, because Africa's mineral assets are its chief strength. The investment can be used to find natural resources through a contract managed by the diaspora company. Profits can be used to pay a dividend to investors, and many economists and engineers, located both in Africa and out of it, can support each other in planning and management. This will help to bring billions of dollars into Africa for development. There should also be an African Development Bank and World Bank associated with this plan.

Free trade in Africa will benefit the African people, rather than giving contracts to the Europeans and Chinese. This will help educated young Africans with job opportunities. When African diaspora make this investment, they must think of it as a charitable contribution to their own home country. If it works, your country will become rich, because Mother Africa holds tremendous untapped natural resources. You must overcome your fears and change your mindset, to change Africa. The diaspora in Europe and Africa must realize that in America, millions of jobs were lost in 2020 due to the pandemic, and it happened in Europe as well. It can happen in Africa, but Africa has already gone through many epidemics, including SARS, malaria, yellow fever, Ebola, etc.— but still, Africa and its people survive. The worst virus of all is white colonialists, and Black colonialists who still open the door to them. That is the deadliest disease that has ever affected Africa. You need to find better treatment and hygiene for that epidemic.

A farmer needs soil, water, and seeds to grow produce; a fisherman needs only bait to catch the big fish.

Similarly, some countries need just a little money to tap their natural resources. Companies like GeoResonance are ready to find and support investors through their contacts for those countries—only you have to pay a little for the exploration. Through their precise exploration technology, the report will produce, to the standards of the Canadian Institute of Mining (CIM) and Joint Ore Reserves Committee (JORC) accurate information about the available quantity of hydrocarbon, gold, and other metal reserves. They will also provide a road map for how to develop the countries, from their associate companies.

Once you have these reports ready, all the investors will come to you with substantial mining offers. For more information, and a consult, contact Sebastian Joseph, Marketing Manager, GeoResonance Company Limited (sebastian@georesonance.co).

All African countries must follow the example of Qatar, which became one of the richest countries in the world in just twenty years. The project was initiated by Qatar Gas together with its partner Exxon Mobil and later included other foreign investors. The project started produc- tion in 1999. The company RasGas was then established in a joint stock company between Qatar Petroleum and Exxon Mobil in 2001. It was set up as the operating company for the production facilities based in Ras Laffan Industrial City.

Qatar is a small country, and it's only natural resource is hydrocarbon reserves. In twenty years, it became one of the richest countries in the world, thanks to powerful leadership with no corruption. The citizens of Qatar provide heartfelt support to their country's leaders. Presently, Qatar has invested in many African countries.

To the generation of young people in Africa:

What are you waiting for? The main thing that the African people and their leaders are missing is confidence, and a strong belief that you are worthy though you are Black. A generation has passed, and yet still a feeling of guilt and discomfort remains in many African people's minds. Don't be afraid of your color. Your parents and ancestors struggled a lot with that—are you going to inherit those fears and pass a slave mentality to your children? Truly, what virtue do the whites or the others have? They are not stronger or better than you.

In the words of Rev. Dr. Martin Luther King Jr: **"In your blueprint of developing Africa, you must say and believe it confidently that we are black but beautiful, and therefore you don't have to purchase cosmetics to make you fair and straighten your hair. Our hair is better than anyone's and it is beautiful; you are stronger than anyone. Don't think of your biological features— don't allow anybody to pull you down so low to hate them again. You must believe that we can be somebody. Black and white are the same; it's nature's claim that nobody can question on the master plan. I must be measured by my soul and my mind, the standards of mankind. It is your responsibility— there are empty stomachs to be filled with food. There are empty pockets to be filled with money."**

Your parents put in a lot of effort to be educated or to graduate from college or technical training, not to be slaves anymore. It is your responsibility to change the present Africa to be better, not to be poor in the eyes of the world anymore. Yes, it is your responsibility to find the thieves and crooks in your country and abolish them permanently. Let the world come to you—the wealth of Africa should not be limited to a few people's enjoyment. It should be shared by all African citizens. Don't allow the colonialists to spoil humanity, jungles, and wildlife for their own benefit.

Always remember that the world is not only for humans to live in, but also for the animals and trees. We are equals to the earth. Africa is rich—its remaining hydrocarbon and mineral assets, and the food it produces, is enough to feed the entire world. As a young generation, your one and only job is to cleanse your country's leadership and throw out the colonialists. It can be done through a students' movement, because it has been proven that students' movements are powerful tools for restoring order. You are the Kingdom of the African continent—let the other continents come to you so Mother Africa can feed them. But you must have a commitment to the eternal principles of Beauty, Love, and Justice, and you must remove from your heart Jealousy and Greed.

Let the leaders of Africa and its people come together to rebuild the African continent. You have a responsibility to make Africa a better nation and to make life better for everyone in Africa. Your slogan must not be "Burn baby burn" but "Build baby build" and "Learn baby learn" so that we can "Earn baby earn." Through a powerful commitment, you can exchange yesterday's injustice for tomorrow's justice and humanity.

Development is not limited to exploration and mining. The first step is to extract the assets from your home country, export them, and bring money home. You will be supplying raw materials as the world demands. Now you can see the sudden growth of your GDP, and then you can focus on infrastructure and basic needs of your country. That means better roads, electricity (using clean energy methods such as solar power), clean water, and sanitation. Africa is blessed with sunlight, which can produce more solar electricity than Europe and the Middle East, because the essential component of radiation, which produces solar power, is much higher in comparison to other countries. You can see many solar-powered airports and factories around the world.

Once the four key components are in place—electricity, water, roads, and sanitation—then all the other businesses will fall into place, such as manufacturing plants and factories that will utilize your country's raw materials to make finished goods. You can supply your country's needs first and export the rest. You will benefit in two ways, saving money by reducing imports, and making money by increasing exports. That's how your economy will expand and improve.

Attract investors and arrange accommodation for foreign companies to come with their technology to manufacture their products. This will also support the government's income with import and export taxes. Additionally, your citizens will get jobs at these factories.

Do not spend money to buy more weapons than your country needs in order to control domestic crime. Your people don't need war— they need a better quality of life. If you treat your citizens well, there will be no violence, since you are not going to attack or steal from neighboring countries. Remember the game—the weapons manufacturers need to sell weapons, and they are the ones creating religious dissent and violence. They are the ones spending money to supply weapons that will destroy your economy. This game has been going on for nearly a century. When they make new weapons, they want to clear out the old technology, so they use these weapons to create violence in your country and sell you only the outdated stock that they no longer want.

Beware: Only you can save yourself and your country. Listen to those who came before you and pay attention to their wisdom; make an advisory board from your educated citizens along with good people from your country, and seek their advice on steps to take next.

It is not advisable to take an offer from a mining company that wants to take all of your precious metals and export them. The meager profit they give to you makes you feel great, because when you see a few million, you may think that is enough—why should you risk more? But this is utter foolishness, a game that has been going on for centuries. Do you think these exploiters would give you any money at all, unless they were making a big profit? Definitely not. If they offer you a million, it is because they have made ten million from your country. Now is the time to take a risk and benefit from your own assets. Once you are successful with one project, then you can utilize the same funds for the next exploration and mining operation.

Protecting your forest and animals is also part of developing the country. They are just as important to protect as your own people are, and they also have the right to live in this world with us. Once your wilderness is well protected, then the tourism industry will expand. Most African countries are blessed with wilderness and animals, but only a few countries use them correctly.

There are many colleges and engineering schools in Africa, but we don't see agricultural colleges. Agricultural training must start at a young age, so that children will learn the importance of plants, trees, and food production. Once they grow up, they will be well trained to develop their own farms rather than looking for jobs. They can become independent business owners.

This is the latest tweet from an Indian leader, Priyanka Gandhi, who lost her father (former Indian Prime Minister Rajeev Gandhi) in a terrorist attack:

"Be kind with those who are cruel to you,
Imagine how unfair life is all around
And to know that it is not so.
No matter how dark the sky is,
No matter how scary the storm is,
No matter how great your sorrows are,
To be filled with love."

Yes, being an African, you must forgive and forget the past and move forward to a better future for you and your generation.

"Strike the iron when it's cold, to make the iron hot."
"Think within the box, let the box break when it's full."

This is the philosophy from Dr. PLO Lumumba. Dr. Lumumba is ab solutely right—Africans are like cold iron, and somebody must strike them to get them hot, to wake them up and see what is happening in Africa and the world beyond.

You don't need to think outside the box now, because the assets in your country are more than enough to make you and Africa better. It is not necessary to think outside the box until you fill your box.

Dr. Patrick Loch Otieno Lubumba is a Kenyan who served as Director of the Kenya Anti-Corruption Commission from September 2010 to August 2011. Since 2014, he has been Director of the Kenya School of Law. An eloquent lawyer, Lumumba holds a PhD in maritime law from the University of Ghent in Belgium. This is not his only achievement, but it would require multiple pages to describe all of his degrees and accomplishments. He is Africa's 21st-century gem. If you are from the African continent, you must listen to him.

During white colonialism in Africa, all the Black people and their leaders fought for freedom from the British, French, Italians, Turkish, Germans, etc. with one voice, one heart, and one soul. Many of them gave their lives to get freedom, and Mother Africa found freedom from white colonialism. But that freedom was enjoyed by the fifty-five African countries for only a few years. Many of the leaders who came later did not do justice to the people of Africa. Again, their brains were controlled by white colonialists. And to this day, this game goes on, with the support of Black colonialists within each country. Nobody has the guts to talk or take any initiative to change this corrupt leadership, with a few exceptions, including leaders like Dr. PLO Lumumba of Kenya and Julius Malema of South Africa.

I admire all the leaders who are fighting for humanity and the real meaning of human rights around the world, and especially in Africa. I would like to recognize the two great African leaders of the 21st century: President of Rwanda, Paul Kagame, who has proven to African leaders that it is not necessary to tolerate objections from white and Black colonialists, and who brought Rwanda up out of poverty; and Dr. PLO Lumumba of Kenya, who has no fear of anyone and has never been bought by any special-interest group—he proclaims his thoughts loudly regardless of whether anyone likes it or not.

I wish I could go to these men's homes personally, to wash their feet and clean their house for at least one day, because these leaders would never take advantage of their position to get even so much as a bouquet of flowers for free.

CHAPTER 16

The True Leaders on The African Continent

If you want to walk fast, walk alone. If you want to walk far, walk together.

Leadership is the key component missing all over Africa, which pre- vents Africans from exploring and controlling wealth. The main problem in Africa is that everyone wants to be a leader, which is not practical and which causes civil war and financial crisis. A leader is the one in charge, the person who convinces other people to follow. A great leader inspires confidence in others and moves them to action. The people themselves recognize him as their obvious leader. But few leaders have made their best effort to develop Africa.

Remember that even the lion will not catch the deer, if the lion is not running at full speed.

Here are some of the great leaders who fought to bring freedom to Africa:

Haile Selassie, Emperor of Ethiopia (1930-1974): Prior to his coronation in 1930, he had been Regent Plenipotentiary of Ethiopia since 1916. He is a defining figure in modern Ethiopian history. Ethiopia was the only country not attacked by white colonialists, with the exception of the Italians during Mussolini's rule from 1936 to 1941.

But even during those five years, the Italians did not succeed in doing anything other than capturing the capital, the present Addis Ababa.

The emperor was Ethiopia's finest leader. His main priority was education; he opened many schools, colleges, and engineering/technical schools. He gave students the opportunity to study law and aviation. He encouraged the arts and opened theaters. He was the education minister in Ethiopia for many years.

"It's us today and you tomorrow!" This was the rallying cry of Emperor Haile Selassie to the European Union when Mussolini invaded Ethiopia in 1930. He used his loving, influential character with the European Union to oust Italy and take his power back.

He was the founder of OAU—Organization of African Unity, an intergovernmental organization established on 25 May 1963 in Addis Ababa, Ethiopia, with thirty-two signatory governments. One of the main heads for OAU's establishment was Kwame Nkrumah of Ghana. Later, OAU changed its name to AU, the African Union, which is a continental union consisting of fifty-five member states located on the continent of Africa. The founding of the AU was announced in the Sirte Declaration at Sirte, Libya in 1999.

The emperor did his best to build all of Africa. He was the main peace- maker among most African countries and communities. He brought many children to Ethiopia to give them a better education. The emperor started Ethiopian Airlines, to connect Ethiopia with the rest of Africa. The airline is wholly owned by the country's government. EAL was founded on 21 December 1945 and commenced operations on 8 April 1946, expanding to international flights in 1951. Later, the socialist movement "Dreg" came to power and assassinated the emperor. Africa lost a great leader.

Julius Kambarage Nyerere, Prime Minister and President of Tanganyika/Tanzania, 1961-1985. Nyerere was a Tanzanian anti-colonial activist, politician, and political theorist referred to as "Mwalimu" ("the teacher"). He governed Tanganyika as prime minister from 1961 to 1962 and then as president from 1963 to 1964, after which he led its successor state, Tanzania, as president from 1964 to 1985.

He believed in equality and treated Prince Charles just the same as a mama in a Tanzanian village. He traveled all over the country, speaking to all the tribal people about independence. He forged a relationship with the British government and convinced them to hold a free election, achieving independence without bloodshed. He studied at the regular school in Tanzania and gave the same education to his children, sitting side by side with ordinary citizens. He never wanted anything for himself; the only things he desired were for his country. Therefore, the military built a house as a gift for him when he won the war with Uganda against Idi Amin in 1978/1979. This may be the first time in history that a military group gifted a house to the president of their country.

He made education a priority for all the children in Tanzania. He supported other African countries in finding freedom from white colonial- ism. He is one of the founding members of the AU. He told all the African countries that without African unity, there is no future for Africa, which is still true today. He died in 1999 and was widely mourned.

Jomo Kenyatta, Prime Minister and President of Kenya, 1963–1978: Kenyatta was a Kenyan anti-colonial activist and politician who governed Kenya as its prime minister from 1963 to 1964 and then as its first president from 1964 onward. Kenya was one of the fastest-growing countries in Africa, with an attractive infrastructure in the city of Nairobi.

Kenya had been colonialized by the British, who ruled over the Kenyan people and treated them as slaves. They labeled the whites as first-class citizens, Asians as second-class, and Kenyans as third-class, and anyone who objected was shot dead with no mercy. The Kenyans were given an identification card which was put in a metal tag and worn around the neck like a dog license.

Jomo Kenyatta was from the ethnic Kikuyu community in the Island, the largest ethnic group in Kenya. He worked to put himself through school. In the 1920s he entered politics and went to Britain for higher education. In 1946, he gained popular support and led the people against the British for freedom. He electrified the crowd during his political speeches and gained a place in all Kenyans' hearts.

In 1950, the freedom fighters were ready to begin violence against Britain. Thousands of people were killed, and Kenyatta was arrested in 1952 and sentenced to seven years of hard labor. In 1962, he was released, and in 1963 Kenyatta's party won the election, and he became the first prime minister of an independent Kenya.

In his final words to the British, he said that Kenya was ready to forget the past, and all British must leave Kenya. He refused to live in the official state house, saying that the ghosts of white people were there, and he didn't want to live in it.

Africa needs leaders like Jomo Kenyatta. He died in 1978 and was deeply mourned by all Kenyan citizens.

Robert Mugabe, Prime Minister/Presidentof Zimbabwe (Southern Rhodesia), 1980-2017:

"The wrongs of the past must now stand forgiven and forgotten."

Mugabe has been a political actor for more than four decades. He was born in 1924, just months after a British colony was established called Southern Rhodesia. He was educated in history and English in Zimbabwe and went on to further study at London University.

He was a teacher in Ghana, and during his career, he influenced President Kwame Nkrumah to support Ghana in being the first to seek colonial freedom. Mugabe declared himself a Marxist while in Ghana. In 1960, Mugabe decided to visit home. He was shocked by how things had changed in Southern Rhodesia—a new colonial government had brought in thousands of white settlers, who had displaced Black families now coming to Harare in search of survival. Mugabe was outraged, and the situation inspired him to change his profession from teaching to politics. He was impressed with Marxist philosophy and their dedication to equality among people.

Mugabe was elected public secretary of the National Democratic Party. In 1963, he founded a resistance movement that pledged to achieve independence by any means necessary, including violence. That movement was called Zimbabwe African National Union (ZANU). This declaration landed Mugabe in jail at the hands of the colonial government for a decade. While he was in jail, he earned two more law degrees and was also busy corresponding with guerrilla operations. He escaped from the colonialists and joined a guerrilla group, which had support and training from the Chinese to fight white colonialists.

After five years of fighting and support from the leaders of neighboring countries, in 1979 the colonial government allowed elections that resulted in a Black government, and the country was renamed Zimbabwe. This government was not internationally recognized. Eventually, an internationally supervised new election was held, and Mugabe was elected to be the first Prime Minister of Zimbabwe. April 17th, 1980 was Zimbabwe's official Independence Day. Two hundred thousand whites were living in Zimbabwe, controlling it, and six thousand farmers owned 45 percent of the agricultural land. Mugabe decided to take action to develop the country, especially in the education and healthcare sectors.

Mugabe served as prime minister from 1980 to 1987 and as president from 1987 to 2017.

Thomas Sankara, President of Burkina Faso, 1983–1987: Thomas Isidore Noël Sankara was a Burkinabé revolutionary and President of Burkina Faso (which means "Land of Upright People") from 1983 to 1987. A Marxist–Leninist and pan-Africanist, he was viewed by supporters as a charismatic and iconic figure of revolution and is sometimes referred to as "Africa's Che Guevara."

This revolutionary leader fought to get freedom from France. He taught the nation to be upright, to work hard, to welcome other people, and that you must love yourself in order to love other people. He is a man who values other people. He has stood against injustice ever since child- hood. He is the only leader who proudly taught his people not to accept aid from the Western world, because he understood what really was be- hind the so-called "charity."

During his military training in Madagascar, he was impressed with the people's uprising, which inspired him to become a leader. He was friends with many revolutionary men, including those from Ghana. In the 1980s, Burkina Faso was hit by many labor union strikes influenced by the French government. At last, the whites succeeded in their "divide and rule" political agenda in Burkina Faso. After four years of his presidency, he was assassinated. Again, the former colonial masters of France took control to manage for twenty-seven years with a leader they selected, to further their political and economic agenda. Thomas Sankara's soul lived on in each citizen of Burkina Faso. With his death, Africa lost a great leader.

Kwame Nkrumah, Prime Minister/President of Ghana: Kwame Nkrumah PC was a Ghanaian politician and revolutionary. He was the first Prime Minister and President of Ghana, having led the Gold Coast to independence from Britain in 1957.

His dream was to see a United States of Africa. A charming, heartfelt man who was committed to Africa, he studied at Lincoln University in the United States. During his education, he became impressed by Karl Marx and socialism. He wanted to bring all the African nations together as one nation with one central bank and a single currency so that the African continent would be the richest in the world in wealth, military, and manpower. He wrote the book *I Speak of Freedom*. He was arrested by the British government during white colonialism in Ghana, but the youth movement gathered together to free him on 6 March 1957, and he became Prime Minister of Ghana. He survived five murder attempts and died in a Romanian hospital in 1972.

Zambia: Kenneth David Buchizya Kaunda, also known as KK, is a Zambian former politician who served as the first President of Zambia from 1964 to 1991

Namibia: Samuel Shafishuna Daniel Nujoma is a Namibian revolutionary, anti-apartheid activist, and politician who served three terms as the first President of Namibia, from 1990 to 2005. Nujoma was a founding member and the first president of the South West Africa People's Organization in 1960.

Angola: José Eduardo dos Santos is an Angolan politician who served as President of Angola from 1979 to 2017.

South Africa: Nelson Rolihlahla Mandela was a South African anti-apartheid revolutionary, political leader, and philanthropist who served as President of South Africa from 1994 to 1999. He was the country's first Black head of state and the first elected in a fully representative democratic election.

Mozambique: Samora Moisés Machel was a Mozambican military commander, politician, and revolutionary. A socialist in the tradition of Marxism-Leninism, he served as the first President of Mozambique starting at the country's independence in 1975.

There are many more examples. These fathers of liberty fought to get freedom for Africa by risking and sacrificing their lives. It was not in the best interest of colonialists to give freedom and independence to Africa. However, these leaders gathered the citizens together to rebel against colonialism, and so the colonialists had no choice but to leave. It is true that during the early days of independence, the leaders guided the people to make the country better, and until their deaths, most of the countries did well and their economies improved. But the next generation of leaders fell once again into the colonialist trap and allowed colonialist agendas to rule the country. Therefore, as you can see, there are no changes happening now in most African countries, and raw natural resources are still being exported to Europe, in return for which they send weapons to control and kill people who object to them. Now there are only a few leaders who are truly working for Africa's benefit.

It is the duty of each young African to learn why their forefather's sacrificed their lives to win freedom from colonialism.

You must realize that it is the white colonialists' political agenda to divide and rule. In early centuries, India, China, the United States, and Europe were controlled by European kings, after they were colonized.

But later, these countries came together to rebel against colonialism. But even after the independence of India, the British did not forget to break up India, Pakistan, and Bangladesh to prevent India from becoming a formidable, large power. Why is Africa not united? This was the dream of those who fought for freedom. They envisioned a United States of Africa—one country, one currency, one race (the human race). **When will that dream come true?** But now there are only a few real leaders, like **Professor Patrick Loch Otieno Lumumba**, who are still sacrificing their lives to see the further development of African countries.

It is not an easy task to unite fifty-five countries. It has not happened successfully on other continents, as well. Priority must be given to the countries who want to unite reven if only ten countries want to unite at the beginning, that is worthwhile, and they do not need to be neighboring countries. Then appoint leaders such as Professor Lumumba, who have the capacity and knowledge to develop each country, and who also have the legal expertise to rewrite the countries' constitution to reflect Africa's needs, goals, and character rather than the colonialists' style. Good leaders who have retired from politics can be appointed to an advisory board, which can share experiences both good and bad. You must not appoint or seek advice from white colonialists, because their advice is not going to be good for Africa—it will always be self-serving. If neighboring countries try to unite, it will never happen on the first try, because colonialists will divide those countries to kill each other, per their agenda to stop African unity. But once the growth and improvements of the United States of Africa become obvious, other countries will join—even if their leaders do not want to, the people will rise up in revolution to join the United States of Africa.

It would make sense to unite the African countries that are presently well developed: Ethiopia, Tanzania, Botswana, Ghana, Rwanda, Namibia, Kenya, Sudan. However, the presidents and ministers of these countries may not agree with this due to fear of losing their positions.

However, they do not need to fear this if they copy the model of the Indian Republican Constitution along with their own African Constitution, so that each country will be established as a separate state with its own constitution under the umbrella of the United States of Africa's constitution. This way, nobody will lose power, and the presidents can unite and create an organization like the United Nations, but specific to Africa, to serve and support the poorest African countries and make one Africa. A united Africa can consider its assets and manage them well—the natural reserves of these so-called "poor" countries can easily support them if correctly used. Then Africa will not need the current United Nations, which is a tool of colonialism. Within a few years, the African continent would be the richest in the world.

PLO Lumumba: Patrick Loch Otieno Lumumba is a Kenyan who served as the Director of Kenya Anti-Corruption Commission from September 2010 to August 2011. Since 2014, Lumumba has been the Director of Kenya School of Law. An eloquent lawyer, Lumumba holds a PhD in maritime law from the University of Ghent in Belgium.

He is a highly educated, uncorrupted leader who is willing to share his vision to Africa and its people, risking his safety and his life if need be. His speeches are full of undeniable positive energy. He is a model of a servant leader, unlike other leaders who want power for its own sake. Dr. Lumumba travels all over the continent, with many countries inviting him to give a presentation. The people admire him and at each conference he does his job perfectly. He has purpose and a vision. That is the duty of a real leader. But although the people listen to him speak and clap and sing, they don't really understand that he is committing his life to unite the African countries.

The story of the eagle and the chickens

Let me remind you of an old story. An eagle felt pity when he saw a group of chickens that could not fly despite having wings. The eagle decided to teach them to fly, like him. When the chickens accepted the offer, they became friends with the eagle. Then the eagle told them, "From today onward, I am your master. I will teach you how to fly. All of you must come to the top of the hill." Per this command, the chickens climbed to the top of the hill. The eagle came down and started training them in the baby steps of flying. As a first step, the eagle told the chickens to jump from the hill and spread their wings. Flying for the first time felt good to the chickens. At the eagle's command, the chickens repeated this action to overcome their fears.

The next flying lesson started from a mountain, and this time, because of fear, a few of the chickens decided not to attend. The rest of the chickens attended, and this time they flew to the ground from the mountain—wow, that was a nice feeling! Now the fear was totally gone from all the chickens' minds, and they became more interested in learning from the eagle.

The third session started, and this time the eagle told them that they would be flying from one mountain to another. All the chickens fearlessly agreed and flew from one mountain to the next. "Wow, this is an amazing feeling," the group of chickens told the eagle. They repeated this, and all the chickens started flying from one mountain to the next, to the next . . . the whole day was fun for them. When the sun went down, the eagle told them, "Now that you are capable of flying, you can go to your own homes." After giving this command, the eagle flew away. The chickens sent the eagle off with cheers and gratitude . . . **and then the group of chickens walked safely down the mountain and went home.**

Yes, the moral of this story relates directly to Professor Lumumba, who is the eagle flying from one country to another, teaching for years and years. In each country, the people are listening but not taking action. This is not Professor Lumumba's vision; it is not why he has spent his whole life trying to train and give energy to people around the world, especially the younger generations. He knows that young people, especially students, can change the world—when a student movement starts, nothing can stop it. But the young generation must realize that Africa is not poor, that you are not poor. The present leaders, and white and Black colonialists, have made you poor, looting all the assets from your country. If you don't wake up now, you will die. There are many eagle and chicken stories in the link below, to motivate you and make you think:

https://www.google.com/search?q=eagle+and+chicken+story&rlz=1C1N HXL.

There is another leader who is especially focused on the potential of student groups for the next revolution to free Africa from the present Black and white colonialists.

Julius Sello Malema is a South African politician who is a Member of Parliament and the President and Commander-in-Chief of the Economic Freedom Fighters, a South African political party, which he founded in July 2013. He previously served as President of the African National Congress Youth League from 2008 to 2012.

He clearly understands the corruption among current leadership, and he is totally against it. He demands that all mining companies must give a fair share to the laborers who work in the gold mines, risking their lives, and free education to all African children, regardless of color. He knows that Africa must partner with investment companies equally for future business and development—it must be a true partnership, not another colonizing effort like the Chinese have done, colonizing all of Africa. His EFF is getting bigger by the day. All the students and the younger generation must think about whom these present visionaries and your forefathers were fighting against. They were fighting against corrupt leaders and white colonialists in Africa. You must embrace their vision of the better life and future that you deserve.

To the younger generation: Now is the time to start owning your own country and take it back from the parasites.

Why Africa Got Freedom

"Colonialism and racism still exist; the only difference is that now they are controlled within the black community."

Ask any African man or woman whether they want a United States of Africa, and 99% of them will say yes. So, what is stopping it from happening?

There are fifty-five countries in Africa today, according to the United Nations. A few countries still maintain the legacy of their forefathers who fought for freedom and have stayed away from being controlled by white colonialists. But the ultimate result is that Africa is not yet free.

African freedom fighters fought for real freedom—not just to create wealth for a few African political families or a few business people. They wanted all future generations to be eligible to enjoy freedom equally. Sometimes the poor African families ask themselves, "Why did we get freedom? We would be better off as slaves under the umbrella of white colonialism, because when whites controlled the countries, they developed infrastructure, schools, colleges, hospitals, six-lane highways, etc. to create a comfortable life. And we used to get jobs cleaning or cooking in white people's houses, and although we never made a profit, we used to get food to eat. But the present leaders of African countries are not improving development or even maintaining existing facilities in their countries—therefore we are struggling for food, the economy is declining, and the poverty level is even worse than it was in the old days."

It is a must that all African leaders and the younger generation read the constitution of their country again and again, because the leaders have forgotten the ethics and values their forefathers taught them. The corrupt leaders must understand the truth that the younger generation is now educated and have all the necessary information at their fingertips. They also see the difference in standard of living between rich countries and poor countries. They see that the bad political leaders' children have a high standard of living and recreation. Those children are studying in Europe and America or in other wealthy countries, living in beautifully furnished villas or mansions. Their pocket money for a day would support a poor family for an entire month or would pay a civil servant's salary for a month. These bad political leaders and their families travel to the wealthiest countries for medical care, as well.

- It is not a credit to you that you send your children to another country to be educated. Rather, it is shameful, because it proves that you are not a good enough leader to build a desirable educational system within your own country.
- No matter how much money you spend, your children will be second-class citizens in those other countries.
- If you are given favors, it is because of that country's charity, not because of your power.
- The children in your country may need government scholarships for higher education, which is good if they can learn about different cultures and languages.
- You must make education a priority in your country, as former Tanzanian President Julius Neyerere did, so that you and your children will be respected.
- It is not a credit to you that when you or your subordinates get sick, you go to Europe or America for treatment. Rather, it is shameful, because you don't have a healthcare system, or you have no trust in the system you do have. If you don't trust your doctors and hospitals, then how will your country's people trust their healthcare system? It is a mistake not to invest in good

hospitals and competent medical facilities. You must not forget the past. If you were not privileged, you would also go to the regular hospital like everyone else who is standing in line.

Young Gambian Pan-African Ousman Touray sends a powerful message to Africans and the African diaspora not to shy away, and to develop Africa. Gambian politician Sidia Jatta encourages the government to use available means to develop the country.

The government offered Touray a full scholarship to study abroad, but he chose the University of Gambia, where he got a Bachelor's of Science degree in Development. That shows his commitment to his own heritage as an African. He believes that Africa is a better place than any other continent. He was inspired by former Ghanaian president Kwame Nkrumah. Touray is presently an inspiration to Africans, who can look to him as a new young leader. God bless Ousman Touray and support him to successful leadership in Africa.

This has become a symbol of Africa: mothers and young girls with a child on their back, carrying 30–40 kilos of heavy items on their heads, to sell on the street.

You can see an example of this in the image linked below—a woman carrying a bag inscribed with the words "I love Africa," with a baby on her back . . . she still loves Africa despite her struggles. But you, the bad leaders, do not love Africa.

https://www.google.com/search?q=mother+carrying+baby+on+her+back+ and+luggage+on+head&r

Is this your idea of leadership—to throw your mothers into the street as vendors? What impression does your leadership make on the world? It is a shame when you travel to other countries in your custom-tailored suits; it will be remembered that you chose to present yourself like this, while your people suffer.

A good leader accepts the challenge of building schools, colleges, hospitals, roads; a good leader makes clean water, sanitation, and electricity a priority, as these are basic requirements for a developed country. If you do this, your reputation and legacy will be honored, and your children can proudly say, "This was built during my father's time in office."

If you are a political leader fifty years old or more, ask your parents the meaning of leadership. If you are younger, ask your grandparents. If they are dead, ask your elders the meaning of leadership, and they will teach you, even if they have never been inside a school. Because they were born in Africa as Africa's children, they know the law of the jungle.

They will tell you that leadership means being a lion in the jungle. Why not an elephant? Shouldn't the elephant be King of the Jungle, being larger and stronger than the lion? But when they meet each other, the lion is still a predator, regarding the elephant as prey, and the elephant is afraid and tries to escape. It's the same between the giraffe and the cheetah. If size doesn't make an animal superior, then what does?

Intelligence? If so, the fox should be king of the jungle, but he isn't—it's the lion.

What are the leadership qualities of the lion?

- The number one factor is confidence. When he is chasing an animal:
- He never believes that he will fail.
- He is ready to take challenges and risks until he achieves his goal.
- He does not fear for his life during the chase.
- He normally hunts animals that are larger than he is.
- He never eats rotten food.
- He hunts not only for himself, but for his dependents.
- He will protect his dependents and his territory.
- When his belly is full, he will not hunt again until he is hungry.

These are the reasons why the lion is the king of the jungle. How many of the present leaders have the qualities that entitle them to lead? Yes, your forefathers had these qualities, and this is how Africa got its independence from white colonialism. A good father and mother make sure their children have food before they eat, and not only that, the mothers in Africa will care for other children the same as she cares for her own— that is the culture of Africa. A good leader will make sure that his people are fed before he eats. All animals do the same, except for snakes. But some political leaders are worse than snakes. It is a pity that most of the new generation of leaders are content with rotting food and have none of the qualities of the lion.

In India, in 2014 and again in 2019, a political party came to power that offered millions of job opportunities and promised to bring prosperity to farmers. The end result is not as promised, and as a result, thousands of farmers have committed suicide due to poverty. Moreover, fifty years of credibility and stable economics in India have been destroyed. This party even spent billions of rupees to purchase their opposing party's MLA's and minister to join their party and prop it up. The people's prosperity is not important to them. Cows are more important to them than humans are.

We must not deny the fact that the previous government lost the power they had held for more than fifty years, due to corruption and overconfidence. Moreover, they had not paid attention to the poor, to farming, or to opportunities per the requirements of the country and the world. Now they are struggling to come back to power by making big promises. They have realized the power of the people when you don't take care of them.

India gave more attention to developing weapons technology than to infrastructure or the basic needs of the poor. And, trying to be number one in front of the world, of course we needed to develop technologies to impress India and the world. But suppose one of those missiles and rockets backfires; it will bounce back and crash into the piles of shit and mountains of garbage in the slums. Who wants to eat a plate of food from a five-star restaurant when one of the items is a piece of shit, complete with taste and smell?

The biggest recent blunder by the Indian government, designed to protect their image, happened during American president Donald Trump's official visit on 24 February 2020. The government spent millions to build a high-rise wall beside a road in a slum area where more than a thousand families had lived for more than fifty years without any assistance from the government. This money was spent for only two days, to hide the slum and the poor people, while the entourage passed through on their way to the conference. That image made headlines not only in America, but around the world. The money they spent to build the wall was more than enough to build houses and sanitation for the poor families—but the wall was what the government chose to show the President of the United States to demonstrate their leadership. This ridiculous wall was supposed to earn five stars and a gold medal, and support from all the Indian people and from the world? Moreover, the prayers of the poor still come as a blessing to you. But to leaders in Africa, image doesn't matter. They still want to seem poor in front of the world.

How long can you hide? All hidden things will be revealed someday. Be truthful to yourself first; only then are you eligible to serve others.

Every election season, politicians make promises. After they win, they forget everything, and if you're still alive for the next election, you can see them making even bigger promises. They spend millions to get their seats, and after the election, they want to recover the money they spent, so they have no time to think about you. If you ask a political leader how much he spent to win the election, and compare it to the official salary he will get while in office, even if he sat in that position for 200 years, he wouldn't make back the money he spent. Maybe you think he won the election with donations from businessmen in his country? It is proven that a businessman will never spend money up front without knowing how he will get that money back with more profit in return— so, after his candidate wins the election, the businessman will influence the politician and be given big government contracts. The poor stay poor, the rich stay rich, and in between, a few politicians will also be rich within a few years.

There is a new trend, post-colonialism. The leaders have found that they can gather ethnic leaders to bring in during the election, to win. This is similar to the European "divide and rule" policy. Ethnic conflict is the most dangerous agenda for any country, because ethnic and religious fights never end, and they are more powerful weapons than the atom bomb.

All the bad political leaders must remember what it was like during white colonialism. Everyone in the country dreamed of getting freedom from the whites, and local people supported the freedom leaders by giving their lives to protect those leaders. Because of those sacrifices, most countries gained their independence. Those leaders were not only true leaders, but the fathers of their countries. They behaved like true fathers, who want all their children to unite and eat and enjoy together as one family. The dream of those freedom fathers was that all African countries should be united as one nation, called the United States of Africa, so that Together Everyone Achieves More (TEAM). Yes, team-work is important to eradicate poverty in Africa.

If you are a bad political leader, you must realize that now, the people in those African countries have patiently waited all these years, believing your promises. Their patience has reached its breaking point. Now, if the people gather together to rebel, there will be nobody to protect you; you and your family will run naked in the streets, and there is a chance that you will be burned alive. Don't wait for that moment to come. Now is the time to think and change, for your own good and for your family. Never believe that you are the only one who will ever hold power. There are many readily available examples of what happens to dictators in the end. Now is the time to change, to protect yourself so that you don't meet that fate.

It is better to stop singing when the tone is good.

The people of your country selected you to manage the country; you are the servants of the people. Therefore, you are paid, regardless of whether you are a president, prime minister, minister, MLA, or civil servant. You have not brought your family property to serve the people; rather, you are paid from the country's assets, via taxes paid to the government. Yes, because you hold office, you can use your power to manage the people and the country, but you must never forget that everyone in the country deserves the same rights and treatment—including you.

It can be seen that soon after any election, the elected officials begin to become wealthier every day. Are they getting rich from their salaries? Of course not; it is clearly because of corruption. The time has now come for people in each country to work as investigators or police to find these corrupt leaders and bring them to justice. The money they are making should be going to each citizen. The wealth of a country shouldn't be reserved for only a few people and their families to enjoy. The children of elected officials shouldn't be studying in Europe and enjoying a comfortable life while citizens and their families struggle to earn a decent living. The corrupt leaders wear caps on their heads and crosses on their chests, and they make a show of prayer after stealing the benefits and assets that belong to the people they swore to serve. What prayer are they praying? Their prayer must be: "God, protect me from the people when I steal, and if You do, I will offer You a percentage of what I have stolen."

CHAPTER 18

To The Young Generations in Africa

The young men and women in Africa must realize that the world doesn't belong solely to anyone. The world is not supposed to be controlled by so few countries that we can count their number on our fingers. There are 195 countries in the world, and all have an equal right to live on their own land and enjoy their own assets. Some countries may have developed certain technologies, but that doesn't make them superior or more deserving of human rights.

Let me remind you of another story about an eagle and the chickens. A chicken farmer found an eagle's egg. He put it in the nest of one of his hens, so it could be hatched. The eagle and the chicks hatched together. The young eagle grew up with the chickens. He thought he was a chicken, just like them. He did all the things the chickens were doing. Since the chickens could fly only a short distance, the eagle likewise flew short distances. He thought that was the farthest he could go.

One day, the eagle saw a bird flying high, and he was very impressed. He asked the mother hen, "Who is that?"

"That is an eagle, the king of all the birds," the hen replied. "The eagle belongs to the sky. We are just chickens." So the eagle lived and died as a chicken, for that's what he thought he was.

Young people of Africa, do you want to die like that eagle?

You are sleeping giants; you are the kings and queens of the African continent. Each of you must awaken the lion power within you, to protect your territory. Sharpen your teeth, claws, and brains to hunt for your own food, and to feed the generations to come. Find and throw out those who have invaded your territory. Your color, caste, creed, and ethnicity are all your internal problems. Beware of the bad religious leaders, those who misled your forefathers like those chickens did to the eagle and supported the white colonialists in looting all your assets. Still they are the ones controlling you, with the support of some of your bad political leaders. It is your responsibility to find and destroy them.

If one dies, another can fertilize. But the bad leaders kill everyone and use them as fertilizer.

If white colonialists were still ruling in Africa the way they wanted to rule, you would still be standing naked at the slave market with chains around your necks and legs, to be sold at auction. Your forefathers fought with those colonialists to win freedom, but unfortunately due to support within the Black community, those colonialists are still ruling over you. You are still their slaves, but the style has changed.

You must clean your own house first, so it is your responsibility to find the Black colonialists within your country. If you leave your house carelessly and the door is unlocked, then the thieves will come. That's what has been happening for all these years—whites came to your home, stole all your assets, and raped your land . . . and they are still raping it.

Enough is enough. The younger generation must start a new journey, so that you and your children will not struggle as you are struggling now. No one is superior to you. You must acquire the maximum knowledge and power to protect your country.

If you don't act now, the next generation will suffer the same way your forefathers did.

LET THAT HORN SOUND!

COVID-19 CAN MAKE AFRICA RICH

GDP Means: Gross Domestic Product

The following equation is used to calculate GDP: GDP = C + I + G + (X − M) or GDP = private consumption + gross investment + government investment + government spending + (exports − imports). It transforms the money-value measure, nominal GDP, into an index for quantity of total output.

Yes, that formula man be too much for an everyday citizen to understand, but every African leader must have at least a little knowledge about GDP. You must realize that your country is rich in natural reserves, which can increase the GDP, especially regarding exports of gemstones, minerals, gold, gas and oil products, and hydrocarbons.

— Have you ever wondered why the value of your currency is so low, compared to the US dollar or European currencies?
— Does it make sense to you to carry gold in your lap and still go begging for charity?
— Do you think that Europe and America have more gold than Africa? Absolutely not. It's all looted from your country thanks to corrupt politicians and corrupt joint ventures.

A country that exports gold or has access to gold reserves will see an increase in the strength of its currency when gold prices increase, since this increases the value of the country's total exports. In other words, an increase in the price of gold can create a trade surplus. That is how the value of your currency goes up. Remember, sixty years ago, the value of the British pound was equal to that of the currencies of the richest African countries.

Former French President Jacques Chirac was told how African gold supported their economy—of course, it is not accessed through proper channels, or Africa would be wealthy by now. Former American President Donald Trump recently issued an accounting of looted money from Iran, Iraq, and other countries by present political leaders, and the total was in the trillions. How much of Africa's money is there? Only

God and those banks know the truth. In a few years, another financial crisis will come and those banks will shut down. Again, the African people will not realize the truth of what is happening, and the looting process will continue....

This story will remind you that people are greedy.

> A poor man prayed to God for years and years in order to obtain wealth. At last, God heard his prayer and appeared in front of him. God asked, "My son, what is your wish?"
>
> The man said, "For many years, my family and I have not known what wealth is. I want to be rich and for You to give me wealth with Your blessing."
>
> God decided to fulfill his dream and said, "The land you are standing on is full of gold. You can walk starting tomorrow morning, and as much land as you can walk across will be yours."
>
> The man was so happy, and he went home. The next day, starting early in the morning, he began to walk, from morning to afternoon. He was tired, but he thought he should go a little farther before he stopped. He was tired and thirsty but wanted to keep walking until sunset to cover the most ground possible—then he started running, and the exertion was too much for him. He fell down dead, because God asked him to walk, but in his greed, he ran to cover the area more than he deserve. This is also a good lesson for those are trying to be number one in the rich list.

I just want to point out the moral of this story to those who are stealing natural resources from Africa. You had better stop and enjoy what you have—let other people live, at least. There will be consequences for these countries who are killing Africans, making them poor, and stealing their wealth. Disasters will come, such as COVID-19, plague, or black fever—or something else that nobody has imagined yet.

Yes, the time has come for Africa to realize its potential and resist the colonialists still in Africa feeding at the trough. No one has brought justice to Africa—not the Americans, Germans, British, French, Portuguese, Italians, Belgians, Dutch, Arabs, or Asians . . . including the United Nations. If the United Nations had brought justice to the African people, then Africa would not be poor. We can see the United Nations peace- keeping force most heavily involved in the Central African Republic, the Democratic Republic of Congo, and Somalia. What kind of peace are they creating there? For years and years, millions of tons of valuable minerals have been exported from those countries—is this happening without the United Nations' knowledge? In return, they throw a few sacks of food and a bit of medicine at the people and claim to be protecting them, when thieves have come to Africa, brutally killed the people, made them slaves, and looted their minerals and natural resources. The same brutality continues today. The African people would be the richest in the world, if other countries would leave them alone. To the countries who are looting Africa: Enough is enough—why doesn't the brutality against Africans stop? Do you still think Africans are not human? The time has come to change. Beware your greed, which will kill you along with your country.

If you put together the natural resources of just two or three African countries, you would see the biggest GDP in the world. All Africans must realize that and stop kneeling in front of your colonizers. No one is better than you are. They should support you with their technology with agreed-upon profit-sharing, rather than continuing with the current model, in which they invest almost nothing in the country whose assets they are looting, using African people only for labor. The African people must be smart enough to control their own minerals and assets, because most of the raw materials in the world are supplied by Africa: gold, diamonds, copper, uranium, nickel, zinc, silver, iron, aluminum, cobalt, coal, oil, and gas. But African women still carry their babies on their backs and work as street vendors, carrying 40-50 kilos of goods on their heads. All Africans must unite and stop this colonialist nonsense.

COVID-19 is a global crisis, but for Africa it may be a blessing in disguise. Thanks to COVID-19, Africans have realized how good their own country is. Six hundred years before, the colonialists came to Africa and scattered the people all over the world. Now God is returning to the people the land of Africa, a land that flows with milk and honey. This is a good time for the African diaspora to come back to their own country and develop it for future generations.

Now is the time to submit petitions to the international courts, against the countries who are still stealing assets from Africa. They must pay back Africa for everything they have taken. Why don't they believe that stealing is a crime? Otherwise, Africans must hold relief and aid organizations to a different standard—the United Nations, Red Cross, Red Crescent, UNICEF, WHO, etc.—and demand that they stop supporting the looting of Africa's assets and stop protecting the thieves. The peacekeeping forces in Africa give protection to colonialists who are stealing natural resources. If any civilians investigate the ongoing operations, the peacekeeping forces kill them, and then blame them for trying to ruin the country. By protecting those countries, how many of them have become rich and peaceful? The present generation of Africans is well qualified to control and advise their own country. Africa no longer needs advisors from Europe or America.

COVID-19 is the first time a deadly virus has not emerged first in Africa. Normally, viruses spread first in Africa and then to different parts of the world. Those who manufacture viruses also prepare medicines before distributing the virus, so that the medical industry can make billions from it. Unfortunately, this virus started in China, and therefore the well-known manufacturers have not been able to develop profitable treatments. COVID-19 is also a planned move by China to sell products such as COVID test kits, many different types of thermometers, cleaning supplies, gloves, masks, etc. We need to be suspicious because COVID was first detected in December 2019, but by the end of December, testing equipment was already available and ready to sell. How did that happen? Were those manufacturers visionaries who knew that COVID would erupt in December? But disaster struck when their secret spread of the virus spiraled out of control. So, Europe and America took up their swords and are pursuing China, because they do not want China to benefit financially from millions of deaths in Europe and America.

The Bible says that he who lives by the sword will die by the sword; again, the Bible says that God will destroy seven generations when a man does evil to others.

Yes, most of the biggest pharmaceutical companies from Europe and America are in on this too—the death rate is climbing in Europe and America, with innocent people as victims. These days, it is profitable to kill human beings. This comes in many forms, including starting wars and selling weapons, inventing a virus and selling medicine for that virus, adding poison to food so that people get sick and end up in the hospital, and unnecessary medical testing and procedures to make money for hospitals. Now, there is no religion, no religious leader, no church, and no priest that can protect mankind from this pandemic.

This is the only pandemic that has not killed many people in Africa. The best part is that Africa has found herbal medicine from their own land that is a successful treatment, but the WHO will never approve this medicine because it does not come from America or Europe. If African people are recovering from COVID due to this medicine, why won't the WHO support it? Western pharmaceutical companies may develop treatments with side effects, but herbal medicines don't have side effects. Western medicine hasn't developed an effective treatment, and millions are suffering. Again, if you don't want to investigate and approve of a natural treatment from Africa, it is because of your political agenda. This is the first time all the African diaspora wish to come back their home,

- This is the first time that all African leaders have realized their country is better than any other for Africans.
- This is the first time all African leaders are prioritizing improvement of health care systems.
- This is the first time the African people have realized they are better than others.
- This is the first time some of the African countries' leaders have remembered their forefathers who fought for freedom from the colonialists and said Africa must unite to create the United States of Africa.

Yes, this is the best time to develop Africa without interference from white colonialists. Europe and America have already decided to get rid of their old people—in Italy, France, America, and other countries during the pandemic, the lives of people over sixty were not considered valuable. Hospitals were even instructed to give the beds of older patients to young people instead. This proves that the earth has its own policy, to balance the good people and the bad people.

At this point, the rich people are not those who have millions or billions in the bank—rather, they are those who survive the pandemic.

**COVID-19 will surely change Africa's economy
for the better, resulting in wealth.**

CHAPTER 19

The United States of Africa (African: USA)

The Organization of African Unity (OAU) was founded on 25 May, 1963 in Addis Ababa, Ethiopia under the leadership of the founding members Kwame Nkrumah of Ghana and Haile Selassie of Ethiopia. At its founding, it had thirty-two signatory governments. One of the main heads for OAU's establishment was Kwame Nkrumah of Ghana.

The African Union (AU) is a continental union consisting of fifty- five member states under the leadership at Muammar al-Gaddafi Headquarters Addis Ababa, Ethiopia located on the continent of Africa, established from the parent organization, OAU. The AU was announced in the Sirte Declaration in Sirte, Libya, on 9 September 1999, calling for the establishment of the African Union

The African Union (AU) is a continental body consisting of the fifty-five member states that make up the countries of the African Continent. It was officially launched in 2002 as a successor to the Organization of African Unity (OAU, 1963-1999).

North Africa

#	Member state	Capital	Area (km2)
1	Algeria	Algiers	2,381,740
2	Egypt	Cairo	1,001,451
3	Libya	Tripoli	1,759,540
4	Mauritania	Nouakchott	1,030,700
5	Morocco	Rabat	446,550
6	Sahrawi Arab Democratic Republic (Western Sahara)	El Aaiún(proclaimed)	266,060
7	Tunisia	Tunis	163,610

Southern Africa

#	Member state	Capital(s)	Area (km2)
1	Angola	Luanda	1,246,700
2	Botswana	Gaborone	581,726
3	Eswatini	Mbabane	17,364
4	Lesotho	Maseru	30,355
5	Malawi	Lilongwe	118,484
6	Mozambique	Maputo	801,590
7	Namibia	Windhoek	824,116
8	South Africa	Pretoria Cape Town Bloemfontein	1,221,037
9	Zambia	Lusaka	752,618
10	Zimbabwe	Harare	390,757

East Africa

#	Member state	Capital	Area (km2)
1	Comoros	Moroni	2,235
2	Djibouti	Djibouti	23,200
3	Eritrea	Asmara	117,600
4	Ethiopia	Addis Ababa	1,104,300
5	Kenya	Nairobi	580,367
6	Madagascar	Antananarivo	587,041
7	Mauritius	Port Louis	2,040
8	Rwanda	Kigali	26,798

9	Seychelles	Victoria	451
10	Somalia	Mogadishu	637,661
11	South Sudan	Juba	619,745
12	Sudan	Khartoum	1,886,068
13	Tanzania	Dodoma	945,087
14	Uganda	Kampala	236,040

West Africa

#	Member state	Capital	Area (km2)
1	Benin	Porto-Novo	112,622
2	Burkina Faso	Ouagadougou	274,000
3	Cabo Verde	Praia	4,033
4	Côte d'Ivoire	Yamoussoukro	322,462
5	Gambia	Banjul	10,380
6	Ghana	Accra	238,534
7	Guinea-Bissau	Bissau	36,125
8	Guinea	Conakry	245,857
9	Liberia	Monrovia	111,369
10	Mali	Bamako	1,240,192
11	Niger	Niamey	1,267,000
12	Nigeria	Abuja	923,768
13	Senegal	Dakar	196,723
14	Sierra Leone	Freetown	71,740
15	Togo	Lomé	56,78

Central Africa

#	Member state	Capital	Area (km2)
1	Burundi	Gitega	27,834
2	Cameroon	Yaounde	475,442
3	Central African Republic	Bangui	622,984
4	Chad	N'Djamena	1,284,000
5	Congo Republic	Brazzaville	342,000
6	DR Congo	Kinshasa	2,345,409
7	Equatorial Guinea	Malabo	28,051
8	Gabon	Libreville	267,667
9	São Tomé and Príncipe	São Tomé	964

The founding fathers dreamed of a United States of Africa. The current younger generation and students can unite to fulfill this dream so that you and generations to come will not beg for jobs as diaspora. You do not need to wait in front of any embassy for their mercy, hoping they will grant you a visa to visit; even if they give you a visa, they will still look at you as a second-class citizen. You must be able to travel with a visa from a country you are proud of, a country that is no poorer than the country you are visiting. Without uniting Africa, economic growth will be more difficult.

Each of you should channel the power of Mother Africa with the speed of a cheetah, the teeth of a tiger, the wings of an eagle, the strength of an elephant, the powerful attitude of the lion, and the self-sacrifice of the phoenix.

May God bless everyone with success and a better future for Africa.